As Far As the I

Forward by Marianna Gockley

In 1963, a healthy, handsome baby boy was born to my eldest sister, Catherine, and her husband, Woody. This was a large and boisterous Italian American family in Newtown Square, Pennsylvania, and Dennis was the last of their six children (enough already, Catherine!). I was nineteen and the youngest in my family also. Along with his other siblings, we made Dennis the brunt of all our jokes—even dressing him up in fluffy dresses. Our collective ability to simultaneously torment and lovingly care for him began when he started to walk and talk.

Over the years, I became a quasi-older sister to this noisy, crazy brood. I considered them just as much my siblings, as my actual brothers and sisters. I've been witness and participant to Dennis's entire life—all the sorrows, laughs, and joys. There have been many joys, not the least of which is the family he made with his wife Patty and their three children.

But there have been sorrows too. When Dennis's vision completely failed in 2013, I was heartsick. I knew there was so much for him yet to see, and so many more of life's fantastic moments to experience. I wanted him to see all of these; but as with so much in our lives, we don't get to choose. I hoped he would find a path to happiness over time.

In these pages, you'll bear witness to how Dennis found his path. At times, it was a winding path, and not easily found; but his humor, the constant support and fidelity of his wife, a loving family, and his own inner strength, brought him to 2021 and this memoir. He asked me to edit this book, chapter by beautiful chapter.

I've learned more about those sorrows and joys, and I've relived so many memories as I was brought back in time. I also learned the answer to my questions: How do you shave (with a razor and shaving cream)? Why don't you have a guide dog (I have Patty, what more do I need)? How do you weed the garden (I feel around for what doesn't feel right)? Mostly, though, I've come away from these months we've worked together, with an abiding appreciation for Dennis's humor, and a great deal of respect for the love and dedication that Patty has displayed over the years. She makes him travel to places he otherwise would not go. She motivates him to live life as best as he can. Patty is a testament to "for better or worse" and the commitment they made to each other. Losing his vision affected his entire family, and they all continue to support and guide him.

This is also a story of the life of a resilient human. I'm grateful to him for offering me the opportunity to be part of the creation of this story, and honored to have been part of his path.

I believe this book can help us all learn to cope with whatever curve balls life throws—and we will all have to deal with loss. This is a lesson in how to deal with adversity. There is always someone who has to deal with more than you do.

Good job, Dennis!!

Prologue

Newtown Square, Pennsylvania, is located about 30 minutes west of
Philadelphia, in Delaware County. That's where I was raised. Growing up
in a three-bedroom Cape Cod with five other siblings, you would think that
we would be on top of each other all the time. That wasn't the case though.
I was the last of six children, five of whom were born within seven years.
There was a six-year age gap between me and my fifth sibling. So basically
I was like an only child, with three big sisters who acted like they were my
mother at times. When I was born, my mother and father had not given me
a name yet. So they decided to let my siblings name me. That's where the
name Dennis comes from. I can't stand the name, and still can't stand it
today. I have somewhat of a lisp, so try saying my name with a lisp--
doesn't sound real good. I was born with a lazy right eye, so basically my
vision in that eye was reduced to counting fingers.   The vision in my left
eye was 20/20. That never stopped me when I was younger. I played all
sports and never let it slow me down. Although, at that age I probably
didn't realize that my vision was that bad. As you will find out later in this
book, I should have paid closer attention to it. Now, *Newtown Square* often
gets confused with *Newtown*. Newtown Square is located in Delaware
County, whereas Newtown is in Bucks County. Often while growing-up,
people would ask me where I live. I would tell them Newtown Square and
they would always confuse that with Newtown. But on January 26, 1996,
Newtown Square finally became a place that people would recognize.
That's when a mentally disturbed John Dupont, heir to the famous Dupont
family, drove down from his mansion and shot former gold-medalist

Olympic wrestler Dave Schultz in the driveway of his house. I remember driving to my parents' home in Newtown Square from where I lived in Bucks County, and driving by all the national news media parked outside Shultz's home. That's when Newtown Square made an inauspicious debut on the national and world map. Then when I told people that I lived in Newtown Square, they knew where I lived and what had happened there. Getting back to my love of sports, growing up as the youngest of six, I spent a lot of time by myself in my backyard and my neighbor's backyard. I was either throwing a baseball as high as I could in the air and then catching it, or playing basketball alone in my neighbor's backyard basketball court. I would announce as I played, like I was the star on the Villanova University basketball team. For hours I would be out there in rain, wind or snow. That was going to be my destiny—basketball, and then announcing as an adult.

My friends and I would play wiffleball in my backyard every day during the summer. So much so that it had a dirt homeplate, dirt pitching mound, and dirt for first, second, and third bases. You would think that it would piss my dad off to have the backyard look that way since he was a greens superintendent, but it didn't phase him at all. I give him a lot of credit for that. Although he was probably just pleased that I was not bothering him.

When I went to pre-1st grade at Culbertson Elementary in Newtown Square, that's when my teacher first realized that something was wrong with me. Well, something was wrong with my *eye*, because something is definitely wrong with my *head*. Anyway, when I would be writing with a pencil, both my hands would be on it at the same time, with my head leaning against the desk. At first my teacher thought that something was wrong with me mentally and she let my mother know. Well, my mother was Italian, so you could basically tell what her initial reaction was to that. She let the teacher have it. Telling her that there was nothing wrong with her son, which like I said before to you, was not necessarily true, but anyway she probably said something was wrong with my *eyesight*. This led to me wearing glasses with a patch over my good left eye in order to make my right eye stronger. Nothing changed though. It wasn't until I got older and had contacts that I realized how bad my eyesight really was.

I played basketball at St Anastasia's in the seventh and eighth grades, playing intramural basketball in the fifth and sixth grades. Looking back on it now, I didn't realize that I was basically playing half the court. Meaning that I only had vision for half the basketball court. My peripheral vision was limited to just that one side making it difficult for me to effectively play basketball at a top level. I remember playing basketball in ninth grade for the Marple Newtown Junior High School basketball team and we were playing the faculty members. I had a wide open layup, and instead of continuing on to the basket, I stopped about 8 feet away and took a jump shot, not knowing that there was nobody to my right side. I got a lot of flack for that from my teammates, but I really thought that a teacher was right next to me when he wasn't. Instead of explaining that I could not see very well out of my right eye, I just shook it off and let them tease me. I didn't want anyone to know that I was basically blind in that eye. I guess it was peer pressure.

When I was 20 years old, I was wearing contact lenses. My high school friends and I took a trip to Montreal, Canada. This is where I met my wife, Patty. It's a crazy story but one of my high school friend's sister was going to college at McGill University in Montreal. The guy that she was dating was friends with Patty. We all got together and hung-out over the

Thanksgiving weekend in 1983. When I first saw Patty, I thought she was really pretty. What made me have second thoughts about talking to her was that her friend was, simply in a word, annoying. So I thought that Patty must be just as annoying as her friend. So I grabbed a beer and went to the Pac-Man machine. I was having an amazing game and just at that point, Patty and her friend walked over to the machine and started talking to me. Like a complete asshole that I was, in the middle of the best game of my life, I simply grabbed my beer and walked away from them. Later on in the evening we went to a German music hall and that's when I finally got to know Patty. I think that's when I first fell in love with her.

We went out on our first date a week later when we came back from Canada. We met at the movie theater and saw Richard Pryor's "Here and Now". I thought I was a big shot when I took out my wallet and showed her all the ticket stubs from the concerts that I attended. She just looked at me and then took her wallet from her purse and showed me all the credit cards that she had. Touché, Patty. Ironically, the first year that we were married, we went to a grocery store, and when we came out this guy was selling something I don't remember, possibly drugs. Just kidding. Anyway, he told me that I looked like Richard Pryor. I told him that is the most ridiculous thing I have ever heard in my life.

Patty and I married four years later in 1987. Two years later we had our first child, Kevin, followed by Emily in 1991, and Bryan in 1993. I still can remember when Patty told me that she was pregnant with Bryan, I put my hand over my forehead and just shook my head. The reason for that is that my daughter Emily was such a bad child. We joke about it now.

I continued to play sports throughout my 20s and early 30s. I can recall at least two times when playing sports that I almost got seriously hurt because of my lack of sight in my bad eyes. One time I was playing first base at a softball tournament and a ground ball was hit to me. Now, the guy that hit the ball was a beast. He was huge. So I grabbed the ball and I thought I had plenty of time to run to first base and tag the bag. Wrong! As I got to first base, the beast rolled over me like a freight train, knocking me to the ground. Another time, my friends and I were playing roller hockey indoors. I went behind the net to get the ball and once again, another beast was ready to plow into me. Because I could not see him, I continued to skate and he rolled over me again like a freight train. My one friend was so concerned that I got hit, that he cheered. Nice guy; still a good friend today but at the time he wasn't on my top-10 list of friends. Sometimes you just have to laugh and shrug.

I would periodically go to my eye doctor to get my eyesight checked. He would check out my retinas and he would always tell me that I had to be careful because I'm a one-eyed person. If anything ever happens to your left eye, you will be blind. Being the idiot that I was when I was younger, I just shook it off and said yeah yeah yeah. That won't happen to me. He also told me that I should go to see him every six months for a checkup. Well, that one also went over my head. Should have listened to the guy; maybe I would not be telling the story to you right now. The following story is my path from learning about my lost vision, to the present day--the ups and downs, the laughter and sadness. No holds barred. Everything you need to know about somebody who has lost his vision and how he has coped with it the best that he can.

Chapter 1 - Vaulted Ceiling

January 15, 1996, was Martin Luther King Jr.'s birthday. That was the day that Patty, the kids and I moved from our home in Morrisville, Pennsylvania, to our new home in Langhorne, Pennsylvania. It was a beautiful home. Our dream home--a five bedroom, 2 1/2 bath center hall colonial in a quiet and lovely neighborhood. Unfortunately, that's when the northeast was hit with 2 1/2 feet of snow. When we moved from our house in Morrisville, we didn't get a chance to get all of the kids' lawn toys from our backyard. So, we just left them there. "You are welcome new homeowners in Morrisville", we said to each other. When we pulled the moving truck up to our new home, the previous owner had emptied out all the trash and left it on the curb. What a mess that was. It took a month before all the trash was taken away. Also, what a nice introduction to the neighborhood by having to shovel 2 1/2 feet of snow from our new driveway. Paradise it was not, that day.

The home needed new carpeting and new paint in every room in the house. We held off on getting new carpeting. Orange carpeting in the family room was horrible to see, but it was still our dream home, right? I got to work and painted every room. That was a chore but I did not mind it. We were living in a beautiful home in a beautiful neighborhood. The house had a brick front and white shutters. The driveway had cracks all the way down it, and had weeds growing between them. Not what you would call a pretty-looking home. It had a lot of TLC that needed to be done to it and we were ready for the job. Little by little, the house started to look like a home. The front and back yards were basically weeds. The backyard had at least 10 trees so there really wasn't that much grass growing. A lot of dirt and roots coming up from the ground. There was a chain-link fence around the backyard, and to our right our neighbors had pine trees that were growing through the holes in the fence. A lot of yardwork needed to be done.

When Patty and I first met, she told me that one day she would like to have her parents live with us. Her father's parents lived with her when she was growing up and she wanted to pay it forward. I did not have a problem with that. In 2001, Patty's parents moved in with us. Her mother was watching our children since we moved to Morrisville in 1990, so we figured that it would be easier for her to live with us and watch the kids instead of driving every morning, since she was getting up in age. So Patty and her mother designed a one-bedroom addition to our home. This way they would have their privacy and we would have ours. They had their own kitchen, living room, and bathroom. They usually went out to eat every night, so having a big kitchen was not an issue for my mother-in-law. Besides, my father-in-law loved going out to eat every night. He had his routine: Wendy's, Friendly's, IHOP, and Squirrels Nest Cafe. He knew the waitresses at each place and they knew him. Each Christmas, he would give each of them a $25 gift card. He was like the mayor of all of those places. They loved him so much.

When my father-in-law was younger, he loved swimming. His parents had a summer home in New Jersey. He loved to fish and this was the ideal spot for him as a child. Now, my mother-in-law on the other hand, was not so much a fan of swimming. She carried-on that fear to her daughters. When my in-laws moved in with us in 2001, we all decided that it would be good for my father-in-law to have a pool for him to swim every day because he had a bad heart. OK, OK. Let's be honest here now, Dennis. I love the idea of having an inground pool as well. So did my kids. They always went up the street to our neighbor's house every day to swim in their inground pool. So, we were like the Clampetts.

Backing up a little bit in February 2001, before my in-laws moved in with us, I prepared to paint our kitchen. Now, our kitchen had a vaulted ceiling and I am afraid of heights--my biggest fear. Someday I should go to a hypnotist and get this worked on. I remember being about six years old and I could not even walk up the bleachers because they had a gap between the steps. I'm not talking about the 10 or 11th step, I'm talking about the first or second step. How embarrassing. I also remember one time my mother took me on a class trip with my fellow first graders to Valley Forge. All of the students got in line to climb-up the stairs of the tower in Valley Forge National Park. I'm in line with all of them. I start to go up the first flight of stairs and my butt cheeks start to quiver. I'm thinking to myself, "pull it together Dennis". Well, I can't take it any longer and I turn around and go down the steps. The walk of shame. All my first-grader friends are looking at me and laughing. I didn't care though. I wanted to get the heck out of that tower and fast. No wonder my dad never wanted to play with me when I was younger. OK, this walk down memory lane is getting me depressed. So back to the kitchen. The kitchen had a vaulted ceiling like I said before so I had to get the extension ladder from our garage. I was on top of the ladder about 13 feet high. As I was trimming the wall at its highest point in the kitchen, I started to notice a whiteness coming from the outside of my right eye towards my nose. At first I thought it was the light from the fan that was causing this. But when I got down from the ladder, the whiteness was still there. My eye did not have any pain whatsoever, so I didn't think too much about it. The next morning, that whiteness was still there so I decided to make an appointment with my ophthalmologist. I went after work and when I sat down in his chair and told him what had happened, he told me, let me take a look at it. I will never forget his reaction, He said to me did you get hit in the head? I answered, no. Why? He told me that I had a detached retina. I was confused. How did that happen, I answered? He told me, you tell me. He then told me that I needed to see a retinal specialist. I made an appointment for the following day. The retinal specialist came in and took a look at my eye. He then proceeded to wheel himself over to his desk and start drawing on a circle in his folder. When he was completed, he told me that I had seven holes in my retina. He told me he had never seen anything like that before and I needed to get surgery as soon as possible. Over the next 20 years, that phrase "I have never seen anything like that before" would be told to me by numerous doctors in numerous states. Anyway, I set up an appointment to get my retina attached. The doctor told me that it's not that difficult of a surgery and that it would take 20 to 30 minutes to perform. This would be the first surgery of many, by one of many doctors that I would see over the next 20 years. My father-in-law drove me to the hospital and I sat in the waiting room with him. When they called me back, I told him that he could go home and I would let him know when I was done. In that pre-operating room, little did I know what was ahead of me. Little did I know that I did not have to get that surgery performed. Little did I know that I could have lived my life without that vision in my bad eye either. I had lived with that bad eye my whole life, so what if I couldn't see out of it anymore. I wish I had a time capsule to go back to tell myself this, but at the time I had no idea. I was just trying to save what little eyesight I had in my bad eye.

When my surgery was completed, Patty and my father-in-law came to pick me up. Sitting in the backseat with a patch over my right eye, I could feel myself starting to get emotional. Patty and her father were having a conversation but that was in the far distance of my hearing. All I could think of at that time was, try to keep it together, Dennis. When we got home, my father-in-law went into our kitchen and then into the addition. Patty walked in front of me and into the family room. I was behind them, and a good thing I was. I almost broke down. I had no idea why I was so emotional. I stayed in the kitchen so the kids would not see me being upset. Remember, at the time Kevin was 12, Emily was 10, and Bryan was 8. I did not want them to see their father cry. I only saw my father cry one time in his life and that was at the funeral of his mother. I walked into the family room and said hello to the kids. They asked how I was doing and I said fine, then I proceeded to go upstairs. After you get surgery on your eye for a detached retina, you have to keep your head facing down for three days or until you see your doctor. That is because they insert an air bubble into the eye that needs to keep the retina flat against the back of the eye. So for the next three days, it was not comfortable. When I watched television, I had to put my head between my legs and look down at the floor. Thankfully, Patty had a portable television for me. After my surgery, a parent on Emily's soccer team called me up to see how I made out. He had had a detached retina in his left eye about a month prior while playing basketball. I remembered how bad he looked after his surgery when he came to his daughter and Emily's soccer game. He looked miserable. So after I had my surgery, I felt miserable as well. There was a joke on the soccer team with the parents, that if I stood to his left side, we wouldn't know that each other was there. We tried that a couple of times and it worked. My vision started to come back slowly in my right eye and I started to feel relieved. About a month later though, my vision in that eye went completely white. I was so confused. What did I do to have this happen again? So, like the idiot that I was at the time, instead of going to Wills Eye Hospital in Philadelphia to get my eye looked at, I went back to the butcher who did the first surgery on my eye and had him perform another surgery to reattach my retina. Bad idea. When the surgery was done, he told me that he had to cut the retina and insert oil. Since he used oil in place of the air bubble this time I didn't have to keep my head down. He also told me that there really wasn't anything else he could do. So like I should have done in the first place, I went to see a doctor at Wills Eye Hospital. He was considered the best retina doctor in the area. Now, out of confidentiality, I will not disclose any doctors' names in this book. The doctor came in and he was a short, gray-haired man and wore a white doctor's jacket and a bow tie. He looked like Albert Einstein but with his hair combed. He stood about 5 feet eight and was slim built. His bedside manners weren't the best, but what the heck, if he could do anything with my eye, I would have Dr. Frankenstein work on me. He took a look at my eye and told me that if I wanted to have another surgery, the chances of my eyesight being repaired would be 40% at best. He told it to me straight, which is what I wanted to hear. I thought about it for a while and decided to get a third surgery.

The doctor had me stay overnight at Wills Eye Hospital. I had to sleep facing down with my head in a pillow with a whole in the middle just like a donut. This was uncomfortable for me because I sleep in the fetal position. So I didn't sleep at all that night. All I did was either sit in a chair with my head between my knees or walked back and forth to the bathroom with my head down.

The patient next to me was admitted because he was hit by a flying baseball bat by Scott Rolen of the Philadelphia Phillies during a game. He was not able to have surgery yet because there was too much swelling in his eye. Patty came to pick me up the next morning. She came at 6:00 a.m. and picked up breakfast at Wawa which was located next to the hospital entrance. They guards at the hospital entrance wouldn't let her since it was so early, she called the room upset, so a nurse went down and made an exception to let her in.

Guess what? That one did not work out either. So, the right eye was gone. It basically had been gone my whole life but it was still a part of my life. It took some time to get over the loss but eventually it subsided and I decided to go on living. It had given me 37 years. 37 years of allowing me to be me. I still had 20/20 vision in my left eye so I could deal with that. So from the time I started to paint our kitchen to the time that I had lost vision in that bad eye, it was three months. In three months I had three surgeries that led to me being blind in my right eye. Time to move on, I thought.

Chapter 2 - Rare Disease

In the summer of 2001, my in-laws moved in with us. At that point, construction was underway on installing an inground pool in our backyard. The process took six weeks to complete, but by the beginning of July, construction had been completed. The backyard was such a mess we had to place plywood on top of the dirt to get to the pool from our deck. When it rained, it was a complete mess. It didn't stop us though from getting into our new inground pool. It probably looked really silly with all of us in the pool, and dirt and mud all around it. But who cared, we had an inground pool!

I had sod delivered to our house from the local nursery. There were high tension towers behind our back yard, so I had the nursery drop-off the sod through our back gate into our yard. It took a long time for me to place all of the sod down because I am a perfectionist. I did tell you that my dad was a greens superintendent at a private golf course, so this is where I got my perfectionism from. When I was 15 years old, I started to work at the private golf club where my dad was the boss. I worked there for five years. I didn't start-out on the minor projects on the course: for example, cutting the greens, cutting the rough, cutting the fairways. No, my dad had me starting out on top. I mean doing major projects on the course. For instance, painting the rocks white. I'm completely serious when I say this too. My first job on a private golf course was painting the rocks white. Let me explain. The 14th green at the private golf course, was near a pond. Your approach shot needed to go over the pond to get onto the green. There was a bridge where you walked over the pond to get to the green. That's where the rocks were. Although I was pretty humiliated by the first job of painting rocks, I painted those rocks really well. They were perfect if I say so myself. For my dad's thoughts, who knew. He never told me I did a good job. I guess I did because if I did a bad job he would've told me that. By the next summer, I was cutting the greens. Two summers after that, I was cutting the fairways with a tractor. It was a very stressful job to make sure that your greens were cut perfectly. Like I said before, this was a private course and the members wanted it to be clean and perfect. Try doing that with one good eye. I did though, and no one ever complained. I recall a time when I was cutting the grass around the trees between two fairways. Now, whenever you saw any member ready to hit a shot, you would have to turn off your engine so as not to distract them. Because you know, these are pros out there. Not. These people were hacks. All the money they spent to play on a private, beautiful course and they were hacks. Anyway, so I am standing behind a tree so as not to be seen so that this hack could hit a perfect shot. Well, they hit a perfect shot all right. A perfect shot right at the tree that I was hiding behind. Like the classy people that they were, they went up to their ball and didn't even apologize.

Getting back to the laying down of all of that sod, it was an arduous task but after it was completed, the backyard almost looked as good as a private golf course fairway. Did I mention that as I was laying down all the sod, my family was in the pool waving at me? That didn't really happen but it would be funny if it did. Can you imagine me sweating and cursing and laying down that sod and my family is doing backflips in the pool. My mother-in-law would go into the pool. No, she didn't. She went as far as to roll-up her pants to her knees and put her feet in the water as the kids were swimming. My father-in-law, on the other hand, never went in at all--not one time. I don't think he even got a drop of water on him while he was watching his dog go outside and the kids jumping into the pool.

So, everything was going great. Patty, me, and the kids we're having a great time in the pool while my in-laws were watching us from their addition. As it started to get hot, we would be in the pool every day after school and work. One day, as I was in the pool, I noticed a ton of black spots in my good eye. I rubbed my eyes because I thought that there was some sort of pollen in the air. It didn't go away. If I can describe what it looked like, it was almost like somebody had poured a pepper shaker into my eye. Of course I was greatly concerned. Patty and I made an appointment with my Wills eye doctor right away. I knew that there was no detached retina involved because there was no white curtain from the outer portion of my left eye towards my nose. This was something completely different and obviously concerning to both of us. My doctor was not in the office that day so we saw his associate. Really nice guy, good bedside manners, tall, with dark hair and tan skin. Basically, completely opposite of my primary eye doctor. When I described to him what was going on, he took a look. What he saw was very disturbing. He told Patty and I that there were a lot of white blood cells floating around. That means that there was some sort of an infection in my body. He did not know if the infection was somewhere else in my body and it was showing up in my left eye, but he wanted me to get bloodwork right away to make sure that this was not the case. Patty and I were both floored. An infection in my body? To make matters worse, it was late on a Friday night. Hopefully, there would be a lab open for me to get bloodwork done. After the bloodwork was performed, my doctor looked at the results and concluded that there was no infection in the rest of my body. The infection was just limited to my left eye. He told me that he would prescribe prednisone. That I would have to take 160 mg of prednisone that day and then be on 80 mg of prednisone for the next couple of weeks until I got to see my primary doctor. The prednisone was for the inflammation in my left eye. He really did not know what was going on so he could not determine a diagnosis. This was something that he had never seen before and he wanted to wait for the primary doctor to make a decision on where to go from there. This apparent indecisiveness on what could be causing the problem was definitely alarming to both of us.

When I saw my primary doctor the next time, a multitude of tests were performed on me. They wanted to measure the thickness of my retina and they wanted to take pictures of it in order to determine the severity of the inflammation . He also was confused about what was going on. This did not make me feel any better considering that this guy was the best retinal doctor in the area. After the tests were performed, he concluded that I had a rare disease called ***sympathetic ophthalmia***. Sympathetic ophthalmia, in a brief and simple description, is an autoimmune disease that caused uveitis an inflammation of the middle layer and of my good eye. My body did not know which eye was bad and instead of attacking my bad eye, it started to attack my good eye. Thus, this was the source of all of the white blood cells. Not good news for me. To tell you how rare this disease is, it affects people who have had a detached retina. The problem with me is that my detached retina was not due to any eye trauma. Meaning that I was never hit in the head while playing sports or doing any other function. My doctor told me that one in 10,000 patients who have had a detached retina due to non-trauma, will inevitably get this disease. So that was the cause of the inflammation, and now the treatment would be massive amounts of prednisone daily. Hopefully the inflammation would subside and the damage to my retina would be minimal.

One of my favorite movies "Caddy Shack". In which Bill Murray plays a greens keeper named Carl Spackler. One of the best lines in that movie, is when Bill Murray's character, says: "*so I've got that going for me*". Which was in reference to him caddying for the Dali lama who bestowed upon him total consciousness upon his death bed instead of a monetary tip. When I would tell people what was going on with me, I would tell them that I have sympathetic ophthalmia, then I would follow it up with "*so I've got that going for me*". No one had ever heard of this disease before, not that I ever thought they would. I was still allowed to drive, which later on in this book you will realize that I drove up until the last point that I was allowed. In all honesty, I probably should have stopped driving a year sooner.

After hearing the bad news from my doctor, I can still recall Patty and I sitting in a hallway outside an exam room. I was devastated and scared. So I just proceeded to cry. And I mean I really cried. So much so that Patty had to tell me to calm down and keep it down. At that point I just didn't care. I was just so wrecked with emotion that I just could not stop. I hadn't cried like that in a long time and I think the whole magnitude of the situation had hit me like a brick. All of these questions started to flood into my brain. What am I going to do? Will I go blind? How can I live being blind? Of course, at the time blindness was not on the table. Well, it was but in the far background. This was what I was thinking though. I was thinking the worst at that moment. I'm not a very optimistic person to begin with so this was not out of the ordinary for me to think pessimistically. Patty, on the other hand, was my rock. She just kept on telling me that everything will be OK. Let's not jump to any conclusions and take it as it comes. As I said before, my doctor was not the best with bedside manners and that did not help matters very much. He had been a doctor for a very long time, and I'm sure at that point in his career he had seen it all and just did not have the heart to deal with people's emotions.

So Patty and I took a very long and quiet ride home. I tried my best to keep my chin up and keep my emotions at bay. When we returned home, I did my best to bite my lip and walk into the house like nothing was wrong. The kids knew something was up though. I can never hide my emotions because they are written all over my face. They always knew when I was pissed off at them and I'm sure that they knew that something did not go well at the doctor's office. Like I always did at that time, I told them everything was OK and hid my emotions and just went upstairs and lay down in bed and cried. Looking back on it now, that was not the best thing to do because they were going through this with Patty and me. I should have included them in on all of this, but I was trying to be a man about it. That doesn't mean a man shouldn't cry, but that's how I thought at the time.

Chapter 3 - Roid Rage

I was taking 80 mg of oral prednisone daily and it was starting to play tricks on me. What I mean by that is, every little thing set me off. Everything. It wasn't pretty for Patty and the kids. There really wasn't anything I could do about it. That shit really messes up your blood system worse, I was starting to lose the hair on my legs and arms. This is a side effect of this drug. Everything is a side effect of the drug. One of the worst drugs you could take. It messes up your organs, it messes up your personality, and it masks all the problems that you have while you're on them. Massive amounts of steroids in your body does not, however, make you huge like Lou Ferrigno or Hulk Hogan. It's the opposite effect. It makes you feel lousy. Food doesn't taste good. It's absolutely horrible but it needed to be done. I was tired all the time as well. I didn't wanna do anything. I was a complete mess and so miserable to be around. And the worst part is that I knew that I was miserable and horrible to be around and I just couldn't do anything about it. I didn't wanna be around me. Who would want to be around me? The prednisone seem to be doing its job though. The inflammation had subsided and it was status quo for a while. This was good news at least.

Driving, on the other hand, was a challenge. Driving in the northeast is a challenge whether you are on prednisone or not. Northeast drivers are aggressive and hardly a day goes by when you don't receive the universal language for, well, you know what I mean. Now, like I said before, I am Italian. 100% Italian. So, I have a bit of a temper. I lose it pretty quick too. I also hold grudges. Not a good mix. So driving for me is a challenge without losing my temper on an aggressive northeast driver. Now, insert prednisone into that mix, it's not good. It really wasn't good. Being in a car with me while driving on the turnpike, on prednisone, Italian, and a bad temper, was very explosive. It was like driving with Mad Max. I'm not that big of a guy--6 feet, 175 pounds. I've been that height and weight since high school. Very skinny. Didn't matter. I could be driving next to The Rock and if he pissed me off, it was Go Ttime. I never got into any fights though, thank God

I was an assistant coach on my son's intramural soccer team and one of the parents had said something to my wife. He didn't just say it to my wife, he said it to her with an attitude. Now, I protect my wife and my kids with my life. They are my world. No one, and I mean no one, messes around with them and gets away with it. Insert prednisone? Well, wasn't good. So, we are leaving the soccer field and my wife hesitantly tells me about the incident with her and this parent. I went ballistic. I mean, I went apeshit. I'm screaming, "turn the car around and let me at him". Patty is pleading with me now, please don't. I'm screaming again with all of the kids in the car mind you, "turn around because I want to kill him". I'm serious too. I was that mad. I'm spitting and screaming loudly out of control. I'm sure it was extremely scary for Patty and the kids. Needless to say, Patty did not turn around the car and thankfully so.

Next game, I'm all prepared to say something to this fucking idiot. All the parents were on one side of the field and the coaches and players for both teams were on the other side. Not this one guy though. He walks over to the other side of the field where the coaches are and stands there during the first half of the game with his father. The father is wearing a jacket that says some sort of gym on the back. I guess that was supposed to intimidate me or something. Thankfully, that day the prednisone was not really at its top peak. I was extremely calm. Which by that time, was very rare. The first half ends and I walk toward the kids' huddle. As I am walking towards the huddle, I stop in front of this moron and tell him, "Must be a big man talking real tough to a woman. Why don't you talk that way to a man?" Well, this freak goes totally ballistic on me. I'm smiling at him. The guy's eyes were like he was insane. Also, his father is standing next to him and he's pointing his finger in my chest. I point to the father and say who is this guy? Again, smiling and almost laughing at the whole scenario. The guy then tells me, "want to go into the parking lot?" I respond with, "what, is this fifth grade?" At that point, the wife of the coach comes over and starts yelling at the two guys to get on the other side. The whole thing was ridiculous. The point of my story was I could have really gotten injured badly. I should have kept my mouth shut, but then that's not what this drug allows you to do. It basically takes all the things that you were thinking and brings it right to the surface.

Patty and I went to Niagara Falls on our honeymoon, so we decided to take the kids there on a an early summer vacation. We parked our car in an outdoor lot and gave our keys to the attendant. As we are walking away the attendant starts to yell that we had not payed. We had payed though and I turned around and started walking back to him screaming that we had payed. He realized his mistake and apologized but, he had no idea he was dealing with a mad man. Oddly enough, we showed the kids the hotel we had stayed in on our honeymoon. It was a quaint inn located in Niagara on the Lake whic was 20 minutes north of Niagara Falls. They couldn't have cared less. The serenity of watching the falls cooled down the savage beast inside of me.

Christmas 2002 was not a good time. Patty, the kids and I were all sick. We usually would go over to my mom and dad's house in Newtown Square to celebrate the holiday with my family. It's one of the greatest memories that I will ever have. The whole family sitting in the basement of that old Cape Cod. The basement with the black and white checkered couch. The basement with tile on the floor and wood paneling on the walls. At the bottom of the stairs, was a picture that my sister had painted. It was of the old clown, Emmett Kelly Junior. That clown scared the hell out of me. Of course, being the youngest of six, my siblings thought it was funny to terrorize me with that painting . So, whenever I was in the basement by myself, some sibling would turn off the light and start making ghost sounds. I never ran up those steps so fast in my life.

At the top of the steps to the basement, were swinging bar-room doors. I never thought of this while I was growing up but isn't it strange that they didn't have a regular door? Anyway, my mom always cut my dad's hair and she cut mine too. My mom also dressed me from the local thrift store. Basically, I look like an absolute mess in all my school photos. Bad haircut and bad clothes. No wonder why I never had many dates in school. One day when my mom was butchering my dad's hair, she told me to go upstairs and get a razor and shaving cream. So I dutifully went upstairs because I didn't want my dad to beat the crap out of me for saying no to my mom in front of his face. I brought down the razor and shaving cream. When my mother was done, she told me to bring it back upstairs. Well, I believe I was like 11 years old at the time and I thought I would shave my face too. Thing was I didn't have any facial hair. So I put water on my face and put a little shaving cream on my finger and I rubbed it on my cheek. As soon as the razor hits my face, I cut it. Now I'm panicking. What do I do? So I put a Band-Aid on my cheek. As I go back downstairs, my dad asked me how I cut my face and I told him that I hit it on the bar-room door. Now, my dad knows that I'm not that tall to hit the corner of the bar room door and he asked me to show him how I did it. So I bring him with me and I walk up to the steps and on my tippy toes I show him how I did it. Wrong move. Even on my tippy toes I couldn't even reach where I told him I hit it.

Getting back to Christmas of 2002. We didn't make it that year but we knew that we would be seeing my family because my cousin was getting married at the end of 2002. When I show up for the wedding, my head is huge. I don't mean that I had a big head like I was cocky, I mean that my head was huge from the prednisone. With Patty and the kids being around me all the time though, it didn't look that bad to them because they were used to it. They saw the gradual progression of what the prednisone was doing to my body. My mother and family on the other hand did not. When I walked in and said hi to my mother, she didn't even recognize me. I had to tell her that I was her son. How sad is that? My mother never did anything quietly so once she reacted to me that loudly, everyone turned to see what the ruckus was about. This brought over my aunts and uncles who also did not recognize me. This made me feel great. Here I am at a joyous event with the wedding of my cousin and I'm trying to downplay what is going on with me. I am a lot like my father in that I do not like to talk a lot about myself. I am kind of a humble guy just like my dad. So me trying to explain what was going on was not the easiest thing to do. I just wanted to show up and celebrate. I didn't want to explain my situation. The hard part was that no one had ever heard of this disease. The conversation was like trying to explain how an atom bomb works. There is a picture with me and my beautiful niece on the dance floor that I will always remember. She and I looked so happy, but what really stands out is how bad I looked. My head was huge. I didn't even look like myself. That's how my mother and family saw me, and I could understand their reaction to me.

At this time, I was also an assistant coach on my daughter's travel soccer team. Now, one thing I love to do is coach. I love to see the progress of someone who starts off kind of rough and then gets it and turns into a solid player. That was the case with my daughter's team. I worked on the defense even though I had never played soccer before in my life. Like I had said before, I loved basketball, football and baseball. They were my sports. Growing up, there were no soccer programs in my area. Even if there were, I don't think I would've played. During practice, we would run along with the kids instructing them where to go. As the year went on, I found it extremely difficult for me to run with them without losing my breath. It got to the point that I was scared that I would fall down and break a leg. I did not want to embarrass my daughter so I decided that I could not coach anymore, and I let the head coach know. This was one of the most difficult decisions I had to make because I knew that the prednisone was starting to destroy my body and take away something that I really enjoyed doing.

Chapter 4 - Eye Removal

This process with me taking 80 mg a day of prednisone continued throughout 2003. In 2004, my doctor brought up the possibility of removing my right eye. His thought process was that if I removed that eye, then the sympathetic ophthalmia would subside and I could retain my left eyesight. This of course was not something that I was even remotely considering. There was no way in hell I was going to have that done to me. Even though I was told that a glass eye would look like a normal eye, it didn't matter. No way are you going to remove something from me. Every time that I went to see him, he would always bring up the possibility of having it done. He would always say, "Have you thought about what I said to you?" I would get so mad and tell him I'm not thinking of doing that, and then he would get mad at me. That really pissed me off. Why are you getting mad at me, I thought to myself. It's my body. It's my decision. This is a rare disease, so you don't know that much about it either. Everybody is different. He was old-school though. The doctor that I went to when it first came up that I was having white blood cells in my eyes, thought I should not have it done. I liked that guy and I leaned toward his decision. He was a younger guy and had seen some of the new science that was coming into play on how to deal with my situation. So I had the old-school and the new-school points of view to ponder.

Since the oral prednisone was not really doing its job, my doctor introduced something to me that really freaked me out. Now, I'm not really a fan of needles and who really is? Anyway, he told me that he would have to give me an injection in my eye. It was called Kenalog, which is another form of prednisone. Basically it was a Cortizone injection in my eye.

Athletes and everyday people get those injections in their shoulders or knees. This however was going to be in my eye.

There really was not much time for me to think about the possibility of having an injection in my eye because the next thing I knew the nurse came in with a container and a needle. I could feel the sweat building on my forehead as I kept on looking back at the table and to the nurse. I'm thinking to myself, you are really going to put that needle into my eye? The whole process was just like the movie, "A Clock Work Orange". That's where Malcolm McDowell is sitting in a chair and they have him looking at a film. They have his upper eyelid clamped and his lower eyelid clamped so that his eyes cannot blink. That's exactly what they did to me before they put the needle in my eye. Then "Dr. Bedside Manners" walks in all nonchalantly, like he's done this 1000 times before, which by the way he probably has, and tells me to relax. Relax? How about you sit in this chair doctor and I'll put a needle in your eye, and I'll tell you to relax! Then you tell me how you would be feeling. He tells me to look inward to my nose and tells me I will be feeling a slight pressure. Now before we go any further. Yes, they did give me numbing drops and antiseptic drops so that I would not get an infection. The guy wasn't that much of a barbarian. As he leans forward towards me, I can't help but think that this guy better not sneeze or I'm done. Then I'm thinking I better not sneeze or I'm done. Then I'm thinking the nurse better not sneeze because I don't want her to make me or the doctor jump--then I'd really be screwed. Then I feel a pressure in the outer portion of my eye. It was almost like someone had put a finger in my eye. It didn't hurt by any means but the whole thought of it was not pretty. Then it was over. A cloud appeared in my vision. That was the Kenalog injection. After the needle came out it still felt like there was pressure on my eye. The doctor said that hopefully this would calm down the swelling. If not I would need another injection in six weeks. Six weeks? Are you kidding me?

The word relax has been said to me numerous times in my life. Mostly at the most in opportune times. Relax is said to me before I get a needle in my eye. Relax is said to me while the doctor cuts off my cast that is from my armpit to my wrist. However, the most ridiculous time that I was ever told to relax by a doctor is something that I will never forget. I was having gastro problems so I went to my gastroenterologist for a checkup. I was told that I would need a colonoscopy. OK, no problem. I get the colonoscopy done and about a week or so later I am still having issues. So I called up my gastroenterologist and tell him my problems. He tells me to come in and he will do a flexible sigmoidoscopy. I ask him what the heck is that? He then tells me that it's no big deal and that the procedure would take less than five minutes. Doesn't hurt at all. So I go to the surgery center that he has in his office and I am wheeled into the operating room. I lay on my left side in a very revealing gown and the doctor comes in to the room. Then they tell me to put my knees as close as I can to my chin. Now I'm like almost 50 some years old at this time. You try to put your knees close to your chin. It's almost impossible. I felt like Mr. Pretzel on the table. So next comes the magic word. I have two people on my left side and two people at my bottom. Then the doctor says to me, relax. This, as he is jamming a sigmoidoscope up my rear end. And let me tell you something, it was not painless.

So the Kenalog injections continued for a while and the inflammation still would not subside. The doctor kept on asking me have I given careful consideration about the eye removal. Each time I came in to see him, I was becoming a bit of a celebrity. There would be interns who would ask if they could come in and take a look at my eye. I felt like a piece of meat. What am I going to say to them, no? They were good kids and I figured that I would allow them to take a look at me., Everybody take a look at the bearded woman in the circus. Step right up and watch the man eat a live snake. That's who I was or at least that's who I thought I was. A freak of nature. There were three other doctors in my doctor's practice. I had one opinion on having the eye removed, and one opinion keeping the eye, like I had spoken to you before. Two of the other doctors came in to take a look at me. One said keep the eye and the other said remove it. OK, now I have two doctors saying yes and two doctors saying no. What do I do? Do I flip a coin to decide? Do I go to a fortuneteller and ask her what to do? I have no idea what to do. I talked to Patty about it and she told me that it was my decision although she agreed with me that getting an eye removal was not something that I should get done. Just the operation itself made me want to throw up. So I am starting to come to the realization that I should probably get my eye removed. But I have one last trick up my sleeve. I ask him is there any other doctors that he knows that I could run this by. If that doctor tells me to have the eye removed than I will, reluctantly though. He tells me the name of the doctor and I make an appointment with him right away.

Patty and I go to his office. Very unassuming for an eye doctor of his caliber. Actually, the doctor's offices were in an old Acme supermarket building. Sitting in the waiting room, my legs could not stop shaking. All I'm thinking is what if this guy tells me to have my eye removed? Will I be able to deal with that? Even if I get my eye removed, will the infection in my left eye continue to get worse? And if it gets worse will I be blind and have a glass eye?

The doctor calls my name and I go into his exam room. The guy stood about 6 foot two and was overweight. Salt-and-pepper hair parted on the side, a really nice man. Made me feel at ease right away. He asked me what was going on and I described to him my ordeal. He was very empathetic and made me feel assured that he had heard of my situation before and had dealt with patients who have had it. The big question I wanted answered was will I need my right eye removed. Without hesitation, he told me emphatically, no! That is not something that you need to have done. I could feel tears building up in my eyes. I almost wanted to jump up and kiss him but I would think that would be too forward since I just met him. Maybe I would buy him dinner later.

From that point on, he was my new doctor. If you are keeping tabs, this would be the fourth retinal doctor that I had seen as a patient. Six if you count the two that had given me their opinion about having my eye removed. I asked him if there was any possibility that I would have sight in my right eye in the future. Now this is important here, and Patty can back me up on this, he said yes. You are a young man and they are making incredible progress on research. There is a possibility that one day you will have vision in that eye. Now I'm wanting to buy this guy a box of chocolate and flowers. He was my savior. I had hope. If you don't have hope, then you are done. You are out of the game, but I was still in the game.

He wanted me to get a different test called Fluorescein Angiography. This uses a special camera to take pictures of your retina. Besides getting an injection in the eye, this was the worst procedure I had to have done. They had me look into a camera and take pictures of my left eye. They would hold a pin in front of the camera for me to focus on. The camera flashed a bright light and it was a little uncomfortable but the worst part followed. They then injected Fluorescein which is a dye into my arm and started the process all over again. With the bright light and Fluorescein dye in my veins, I started to get nauseous. Most times I would have to take a break because I was close to throwing up. This gave my doctor several options to view and track my disease.

Chapter 5 - Painful Rainbow

To go along with the 80 mg of prednisone that I was taking daily, my doctor included an anti-autoimmune drug. His thought process was if he could suppress the immune system in my body, then maybe the uveitis would improve. So he told me to see a rheumatologist. The drug that was prescribed for me made everything that I ate taste like aluminum foil. I could recall Patty and I going to a movie and then going to an A&W restaurant in the mall for dinner afterwards. Now, I love birch beer. I also love a good burger. This was going to be a treat for me. However, this was when I first started to take this medication. Predictably, the meal did not go very well. I was so annoyed that I just didn't finish. So now I am on prednisone and this immune suppressant drug, and I don't feel like eating even though I'm hungry. Make sense?

I continue to drive into work. It took me about 25 minutes each morning. While driving into work one day, I started to notice a little cloudiness and a blur in my good eye. This made working quite a chore. I was looking at a computer screen for about 7 1/2 hours a day. Trying to roll my eye around so that this blob that was in my central vision would go away so I could read the computer screen. The doctor informed me that the blob in my eye was due to the vitreous gel and filaments accumulating in my vision. Nothing to be alarmed about. The whiteness was due to a cataract. He did not want to remove it at that point because there was no real reason to do it and he wanted to avoid any surgery at all cost. So I continue to work like this and drive every day for about a year. Looking at the computer screen and rolling my eye around to get the blob out of my central vision was giving me a headache. Not very pleasant. Also, I had started a new job at my company. That was very stressful to begin with and then add on top this new obstacle in my vision. When winter arrived, driving home on the turnpike in the snow was becoming a nightmare. I could recall driving home one day from work and could barely see the car in front of me. With the blowing snow appearing in my headlights, not to mention the cataract in my vision, my driving was almost impossible. The turnpike was never a good place to drive in any type of weather-- rain or snow. On this particular day, the snow had accumulated quickly on the road and made it extremely difficult to drive even for someone with perfect vision. Someone like me and my vision that day, was a recipe for disaster. So I took my time driving in the right lane. Just praying that I would make it home safely. Not a very smart thing for me to do. I white-knuckled it all the way home. Pulling into my driveway, I let out a big sigh of relief. I had made it home safely. Barely. I should've just stop driving then. I should've just thrown the car keys to Patty and said that's it, I'm done. No more driving for me because I'm afraid I'm going to get killed or kill someone else. Did I do that? No, of course not. I'm a stubborn Italian, remember? So I got up the next morning and drove into work in the same type of conditions. This went on for quite a while. Eventually, the decision for me not driving would be made shortly.

When I first got my drivers license, I drove my mom and dad's Caprice Classic down to the old Spectrum in Philadelphia to see Bruce Springsteen and the E St. Band with my friend. That was when the old Spectrum had a third level that was constructed after the building was erected. Now, I had seats in that third section in the last row. I could only see half the stage from where we were seated. I didn't even see Springsteen. It didn't matter though. I was seeing The Boss in concert, and the legendary E St. Band as well. What a great night. I will never forget it. About one month later, my friend and I got tickets to see Tom Petty and the Heartbreakers at the Spectrum once again. This time we had better seats. We were walking through the crowded concourse and I had a soft-serve vanilla ice cream cone in my hand. Now I'm like 17 at the time and I am built like a nail file. My friend is two years younger and built similarly. So I'm happy as a clam eating my ice cream cone and this guy walks the other way and proceeds to put his index finger right into my cone. Whomp. I'm dumbfounded. I can't believe this jerk-off did this to me. Should I turn around and throw it at him. Should I plop it on top of his head and tell him to go screw himself? Nope! I just keep on walking the other way because I am afraid that he will beat the crap out of me if I do anything. In 1982, I got my dream car. A Honda Accord sedan with brown exterior and tan interior. It was beautiful. Five speed. The horn was a button on the steering wheel. So I'm not really used to this car. One day I am making a left hand turn and I turn the steering wheel and I hear someone honk the horn at me. I turned around to see who did it because I know that I didn't do anything to have him honk his horn at me. I continue to drive and I come to another intersection. As I am turning the steering wheel to the left, once again I hear someone honk the horn. Now I'm getting really pissed off. I'm thinking to myself what the hell am I doing to make someone honk the horn at me. Then it dawns on me. I am hitting the button with my thumb and it's me that's making the honking noise. Dumb ass that I am.

That's not the most embarrassing thing that ever happened to me with my 1982 Honda Accord. When I was about 20 years old, I started to work at a tennis center at another private golf course in the area. The thought of bringing the story up again makes me cringe. It's a doozy. So remember when I said that I had a five speed, right? So when you turn off your car with a manual transmission vehicle, you need to pull up the emergency brake as well as keep the car in first gear. This way the car will not roll forward. Well, I pull up to the center, park my car, and go inside. Inside the center, there was a window that overlooks the parking lot. One of my friends was with me that day. From the window in the center, you could see my car. It looked awesome. Raised white letter tires and it had been completely washed and waxed. Well, my friend says to me, your car is rolling down the hill!!. I think the guy is kidding with me and I respond with, yeah right. He tells me that he's not joking so I run to the window to take a look. At that point, I noticed my car going through a fence that was surrounding a clay tennis court and right onto the court. Thankfully, it was winter time and the court did not have a net. Interestingly enough though, my car stopped at center court. Yup. There is my beautiful 1982 Honda Accord stopped right at center court. I had forgotten to put the car in gear. I'm freaking out. The golf course workers needed to come with the front-end loader to pull up the chain link fence to get my car off the court. Most embarrassing moment of my life.

Getting back to me and my driving. I bring up those stories because these are the memories that I have of my car and of driving. Not great memories, but they were memories nonetheless. Made even thinking about not driving such a difficult decision to make. I continued to drive though. Still not at the point to let go.

When it got too difficult and too painful to work and drive with this whiteness and blob in my vision, my doctor suggested I get cataract surgery done. This would take out the cataract, put in a new lens and remove the vitreous gel from my eye. I was laying down on the operating table and I can remember the anesthesiologist telling me to count backwards from 10. At that point, my doctor came in and told me that it won't take that long, and when I woke up he would talk to me about the surgery. Guess when I woke up? At the end of the surgery. while still in the operating room! The doctor is a little freaked out by this. He tells me that he is almost done and not to worry. I didn't feel a thing though. I still was a little woozy from the medication they had given me. Thinking about it now still gives me the willies.

The surgery was a success and afterwards I did not need to wear glasses. It was awesome. I finally had clear vision. I was absolutely ecstatic. I drove into work the next morning and I was a new man, smiling with relief and joy. I figured that the worst was over. I was wrong. About two days later, I am in my boss's office for a meeting, and I start to get severe pain in my left eyeball. It is the worst pain I have ever experienced in my life. It was like somebody had put a clamp on the left side of my head and pushed it inward. At that point, I started to see a rainbow in my vision. It was excruciating. It made me want to scream, but I bit my lip and continued on with the meeting until it was done. Then I called Patty and told her that I needed to go to the hospital because it was an emergency. She picked me up from my office and drove me to the hospital. My doctor was not in that day so another associate of his took a look. Most people have a pressure in the low teens in their vision. That is normal. When I was taking all this prednisone orally, it would mess-up the pressure in my eye so that the pressure reading would be in the high teens. That's not good news for someone because that could lead to glaucoma. Well, when Patty and I got to the hospital, I was hunched over and in so much pain. The doctor took a look at me and told me that the pressure in my eye was at 52. That's freaking horrible. Pressure that high will cause you to have glaucoma and other issues related to your optic nerve. Patty and I were set to go away to Vermont with our family and my friend's family. Needless to say, I was a little alarmed about what was going on with me, and would we be able to still go on our trip. This doctor was really cool though. He was very reassuring and told me that he would not leave the office until my pressure went down. At this time of day, it was close to 6 PM. This guy was the best. Salt-and-pepper haired Irishman. I was wishing that I had gone to see him instead of the first Doctor No Bedside Manners. After about an hour or so of giving me pressure drops, the pressure went down to 28 and I was free to go home. The doctor prescribed pressure drops in addition to the ones I was already taking, I thanked him profusely and he shrugged it off like it was nothing. Now that's a doctor. He could have gone home and spent the night with his family or gone out to dinner with his colleagues, but he chose to be there for Patty and me to make sure that I was safe and sound. I will never forget his generosity.

We made it to Vermont the following weekend with my friend and his family. With my new vision and upbeat attitude, it was an enjoyable trip. We stopped off in a small town in New York for the night. Then we went into this local bar and had dinner and beer. Now I am not that great of a pool player. My brother-in-law will attest to that. On this night though, with my new vision, I was like Minnesota Fats sans the fats. More like Minnesota Slim. I hit every shot imaginable, from every angle imaginable. My friend was joking with me that I was the bionic man. After each shot that I made, I would sing into the pool stick like it was a microphone and I was Elvis. That didn't happen but how cool would that have been?

We made our way to Vermont and guess what? It was the spring and we were prepared to go skiing. Now me and Patty and the kids are not skiers, but we were going to rent ski equipment and go on the bunny hill after a lesson. My friend and his family, on the other hand, were not novice skiers.

They were all set to do some skiing for the weekend. Unfortunately, the ski resort was closed. They had closed it two days prior. Little did Patty and I know this. My friend was none too happy with us. We decided to make the best of it though. One day coming home from a day trip, his wife decided that it would be quicker to go between the mountains than to go around them. Now mind you this is April in Vermont. Little did we know that it was mud season. After a treacherous and afterwards funny ride to think about, we made it between the mountains. Basically we were all driving in vans.

We stopped in Cooperstown, New York, to visit the Baseball Hall of Fame. Walking through the room of plaques of all the all-timers, I would stop and read each one of them. It took me a long time to do this. I can't tell you how many times I stopped, read the plaque, and then turned around and walked into someone. Each time I did this, I would apologize and the person would shake their head because they did not realize that I was not doing this on purpose. Who cares though... I had my vision back. Or so I thought at the time.

Chapter 6 - Don't Tell Mom

I continued to drive back and forth to work every day, not experiencing any problems whatsoever. I took my kids to their sporting events, concerts, and school plays. I drove the one hour to my mom and dad's house once a month to either celebrate a birthday, a holiday, or just to go over to see them. That Cape Cod house was still a very special place for me. It brought back great memories of when I was a child-- running around in the backyard chipping golf balls to imaginary golf holes, standing at the top of my backyard and picking up pine cones and hitting them with a wiffleball bat. If a pine cone landed on the roof of our kitchen, it was a double. If it landed on the roof of our house, it was a triple. If it went completely over the house, then it was a home run. I never really took into consideration what would happen to me if the pine cones hit a window. Dumb ass.

When we would drive back home to our house in Langhorne, Patty and the kids would fall asleep the whole ride home. I didn't care though. I would just put on my Bruce Springsteen CD and sing along with the words while they snored. Not a care in the world. With a smile on my face, I was in control and protecting my family while they slept.

When we were dating and first married, Patty almost always fell asleep while I was driving. This however was not limited to just driving in the car. Patty actually fell asleep in a bar while we were listening to a Bruce Springsteen cover band. She also fell asleep at the old Spectrum while at a Bryan Adams concert. Patty could fall asleep anywhere. Narcolepsy much?

At the beginning of 2006, it started to get much more difficult for me to see while driving. I kept this to myself though. I wanted to keep driving because I knew that once the car keys were taken from me, it would be a difficult pill for me to swallow. No one will ever forget the first time that they took a car out on the road by themselves after receiving a driver's license and the freedom that came with it. I recall when I first got my Honda Accord, I would go to McDonald's every Sunday for breakfast. Same thing every week--pancakes and a sausage patty. I would cut up the pancakes and sausage, then I would pour syrup on top of it, and go to town with my Philadelphia Inquirer sports page on the table. Of course, I should have been at church at that moment, which is where my mother believed I was, but then one week she decided to go to the same mass that I supposedly was going to. I wasn't there though. When she got home, she asked me where I was. I told her I was standing in the front on the left side. She then asked me what the homily was about. She was relentless in her pursuit of the truth. She was like Perry Mason and I was one of her witnesses sitting in a folding chair with a light blinding my face. I stuck to my guns though and she believed me. Maybe she knew I was lying and let me off the hook.

One time I was driving my son Bryan and his friend to a soccer game about 40 minutes away. At this point, I could not read the street signs. I could see if the light was red, yellow, or green, but reading a street sign was getting almost impossible to do. I picked up my son's friend and we started to go to their soccer tournament. While driving down the road, I was trying to figure out which street I was supposed to turn on. So nonchalantly, I asked Bryan if he could read the street signs to me. He dutifully did, and then I came to the street where I was supposed to turn. He had no idea that I could barely see the street sign. He was too busy talking to his friend in the back. We got to the soccer tournament and Patty and Emily met us there. After the tournament was over, I took Bryan and his friend back home. However, this time I didn't need to ask Bryan to read the street signs for me because I know where I was going.

Another time, Emily was at her friend's house in our neighborhood. It was dusk so it was somewhat difficult at that time for me to see. I pulled into her friend's driveway and Emily got into the car. We started talking about soccer. We always talked about soccer. Well, I talked about soccer and Emily listened. More than likely I was probably complaining to her about her play. Anyway, I was talking with my hands, like most Italians do, and not realizing that the car was drifting to the left. At that point, Emily told me to look-out because I was ready to hit a parked car. I quickly turned the car to the right and slightly hit my sideview mirror with the sideview mirror of the parked car. With my heart racing, I put the car in park and got out to see if there was any damage done to my car or the parked car. Thank God, there was no damage to either. Getting back into the car, I glanced over at Emily and tell her the following: "*don't tell mom*". Emily didn't-- not until she was 27 years old. If she had told Patty, I knew that my driving days were over, and I was not ready to call it quits.

In June 2007, Patty, the kids and I went down to Myrtle Beach, South Carolina, with friends and family of ours from Emily's soccer team. Before the trip I went to see my doctor because I was having difficulty. He told me it was just dry eye and to use wetting drops. I knew it was more than that but who am I to question his diagnoses. We did not have a van or SUV though. At that time, we had a charcoal gray Chevy Impala. It was a beautiful car but it was a tight squeeze for my growing children in the back seat. Trying to put all our luggage in the car was a difficult task, but Patty bought a bag to put on top of the roof. So with the kids packed in the back seat like sardines, our trunk filled to the max with luggage and food, the roof rack filled with beach chairs and boogie boards, on we went. We met our friends at their house at 2 o'clock in the morning. It was a 10-hour drive and we wanted to get past the Washington DC area before morning when it gets crowded. By this point, Patty was driving all the time when I was in the car. I felt more comfortable with her driving and so did she. I would take turns with the kids and sit in the backseat watching DVD shows of the Family Guy.

As we got closer to our final destination, it started to rain cats and dogs. It was like a monsoon. All of a sudden, water starts to come into the car. The metal clips that were holding down the beach chairs and boogie boards on the roof, had left a little bit of a gap between the roof and the doors. We had empty water bottles in the car, so we all put the water bottles up against the window to collect the stream of water that was coming into our vehicle. It was really funny. We thought, what a great way to begin our vacation.

The house where we stayed was located in a gated community. It allowed all vacationers a chance to rent a golf cart for the week. That has always been a dream of mine. Own a golf court and drive through the neighborhood. Anyway, we did not rent a golf cart that week. Maybe another time.

One day while I was in the water, I started to notice a little bit of a haze in my vision. At first, I thought that it was the humidity in the air, but then as I continued looking I noticed that I couldn't see the people on the beach. This was not good news. This was on a Tuesday and we still had until Saturday before we went home. What should I do? Well, I went back to the group and pulled my chair up to the water and sat down. Whenever I went to the beach, this is what I always did. It was my favorite thing to do. I put my chair down near the water's edge and just let the water hit my feet while my chair crumpled under the wet sand. This was not one of those moments though. This was a bad moment. Not to mention the people that we were staying with that week had no idea why I moved my chair away from them to the water. They probably thought I was being a prick. I didn't tell them what was going on because I did not want to ruin their vacation. Patty came up to me and asked me what was going on. I told her that my vision was not good and that I was concerned. She asked me if I wanted to go back to Philadelphia to get my eye checked out and I told her no. Maybe it was just a bad day for me, and tomorrow would be better. Tomorrow was not better. Tomorrow was worse than the day before. Vision was just completely white. If I could explain what was going on with me, it was like trying to look through a glass of milk that was diluted with water.

We went to the beach on Wednesday but I just sat near the water's edge again…not speaking to the family that we went down with. They probably thought that I was mad at them but I didn't care. I was trapped in my own self pity and just wallowing in the moment. That night, they asked if we wanted to go out with them for dinner. I told him that I didn't want to. Instead, I just wanted to be alone with Patty and the kids. I was miserable. The kids and Patty played miniature golf while I just walked around and followed them. I tried to put my best face on but I just couldn't do it any longer. Finally, I told Patty that I wanted to go home and get my vision checked out. She was none too pleased with me because it was a 10-hour drive back, but I just couldn't do it anymore. So we told the family that we were staying with that we were going home and what my problem was. I really don't think that they believed that was the problem. I really believe that they thought that I was just pissed-off at them and wanted to get away, but that was not the case.

So with Patty driving, Bryan in the front seat. and me, Kevin and Emily in the back, we took the long journey back to Pennsylvania. Patty stopped along the way to pick up a bag of Skittles that would keep her awake. Not knowing what was wrong with my vision, I was just completely heartbroken.

The following Monday, Patty drove me to the hospital to see my doctor. He told me that there was inflammation in my vision once again. There was this new procedure that was being done for patients who were constantly getting injections in their eyes. What this new procedure did, was to insert a plastic capsule filled with prednisone into a patient's eyes. This would isolate the prednisone to just your eyes and would eliminate getting any more injections. I would no longer have to take oral prednisone. The issue once again was that I am a one-eyed patient and the risk of surgery was always an issue with me. I decided to get the surgery performed and this time I did not wake up while the procedure was being done. The plastic-filled prednisone is called Retisert. It worked just as it was supposed to. It eliminated my inflammation, but it kept me out of work for nine months.

When I returned to work, Patty drove me. She was working about 20 minutes away from me, so like the great person that she is, she dropped me off at work and then continued on to her job. Then she would pick me up from work and we would drive home together.

When I returned to the office, someone had left an eye chart on my desk. I thought it was hysterical but some people thought that it was not in good taste. My vision was obviously not as good as it was before I went out on disability. My doctor's nurse had suggested Zoom Text. This was a computer program that magnified the screen. It helped me out greatly, but initially it was a source of extreme frustration. The job that I was doing, needed two screen monitors. This way, I was able to bring up two different screens at the same time to make the job go quicker. With me using the software, it enlarged the text on the screen so it took up both monitors. Thus, it made my job slower to perform and also made the computer slower to respond to what I was doing. No one in the company that I was working for had ever heard of Zoom Text, so it was difficult to get the ball rolling. Whenever I encountered a problem, having some computer whiz try to fix it was a nightmare.

There were five people doing the same job as I was, and each month we had to meet quality and quantity percentages and numbers. Try to keep up with four other people who have the advantage of two screens being open at one time, me only having one screen open, plus the slowness of my computer, figure out who was the fifth person out of five each month! It was always brought up to me at each of my monthly meetings that I was the fifth one out of five. I tried my hardest not to freak out. Thank God I was not on prednisone at the time because I think I probably would've ripped my shirt off like the Hulk and turned green. I explained to them the reasoning for my fifth placement, but to no avail. They just could not understand, or didn't want to understand. I felt like telling them, "try to sit at my desk at my screen, close one eye, and then try to perform". Good luck with that. It was a struggle. Back and forth every month. I mostly kept to myself at that point. Didn't interact with many of my coworkers. I was just a miserable SOB.

I would get into the office at 6 AM, go to the gym and work out for an hour then get dressed and go to work. Work from 7 AM to 3 PM and then go and sit and wait for Patty to pick me up. We got much closer during that time by talking-out all our issues and understanding each other better. She would tell me about her day and I would tell her about mine. Her frustrations with her job mirrored the same frustrations of mine. I was done driving. Like I had said before, I should have stopped driving about two years earlier but my pride always got in the way. Sideswiping a sideview mirror of a parked car in my neighborhood did not stop me from driving, being unable to read street signs didn't stop me from driving. driving home in a blinding snowstorm on the turnpike didn't stop me from driving. Through it all though, Emily kept her promise. She didn't tell mom.

Unfortunately though, the friends that we went down to Myrtle Beach, South Carolina with aren't our friends any longer. They stopped talking to us. We never found out why, but I would surmise that they thought that I was a prick and they did not believe my disability. That however was not the case. I never saw them again but Patty ran across the mother at a soccer tournament when Emily was on another soccer team. It was a little uncomfortable for Patty. As I learned along my way, friends seem to go away when I was not around anymore.

I went in to my manager's office and told him that I wanted to work full-time at home. At this point, everyone at my office was allowed to work from home two days a week. When I worked from home, I was using a 46-inch TV screen. This worked perfectly with my Zoom Text. Even though I was still only able to use one task at a time, I did not have to deal with the frustration of being around my fellow employees. My manager told me that he was not too keen on the idea of me working at home full-time. He told me that it was against the company's guidelines. I knew someone who was above him, and I asked my manager if I could approach the subject with him. He reluctantly said yes and I went to his boss's office. Now this guy was a really great man. I will never forget his kindness. He told me that he was well aware of the Americans with Disabilities Act and that I could work from home just as long as I kept up my monthly numbers. I went back to my manager and let him know what his boss told me and he just shook his head.

I remember one time I was taking a training class in another wing of our office building. When I got into the room, I made sure that I sat in the front row. This way I thought I would have no difficulty seeing the screen. It didn't work though. With the trainer teaching us a new function, I could not read my computer screen or the big screen in front of the room. I knew the trainer, so afterwards I went up to her and asked her if it would be OK if she came to my desk to show me instead. Another coworker in the back asked me, "why don't you go back to your desk and put your computer in a cart and bring it to the training room?". I told him that I was not going to do that. They need to make accommodations for me, not make me be the one doing the accommodating. When I went back to my desk during the break, I went into my manager's office and told him the deal that I had made with the trainer. Instead of understanding what I was going through, he told me that he didn't want me to complain or make excuses if I struggled with the new system. My father would always close his eyes, shake his head, and grind his teeth to prevent himself from getting out-of-control mad at his children. To this day, I do it and my kids do it too. My sister and brother and their kids do it. Hopefully one day, my grandkids will do it as well. After my manager told me that, I did exactly what my dad did when he got mad. I closed my eyes, shook my head, gritted my teeth and probably turned bright red. I didn't turn green though.

I still couldn't understand why my manager did not get it. His office had glass windows. My desk was just outside his office, so he could see how large the writing was on my screen.

I got my wish and started to work five days a week from home. I sat on a foldable beach chair at a two- foot-high foldable desk, with my stereo on while listening to the Preston and Steve Show every day. During the winter when I was done working, I would start a fire. Sitting at a chair next to the fire, I would watch the flames. It was so peaceful for me. That was my time to get away from my work problems as well as my vision problems. Our family room would get so warm from the fireplace, that by the end of the night I was sitting in my underwear. I loved it.

When Patty would get home from work, I would start up the grill. I loved doing that--standing on the deck with the breeze blowing in my hair, listening to the birds in our backyard, and hearing the water flow around our in-ground pool. It was paradise. This continued until the summer of 2011.

Chapter 7 - Emerald Lake

In 2009, Patty, the kids and I went to Denver, Colorado, for a vacation. While sitting in the airport terminal outside our gate, my vision started to turn all white again. I started to freak-out. I told Patty what was going on and that I didn't want to get on the airplane. She told me there was no way that we were not going on vacation. I felt like I was on the verge of having a nervous breakdown. Just the thought of getting on a plane, going on vacation, and then having to worry about my vision being all white just like it was in South Carolina, was making me freak-out a little bit.

The whole plane ride to Denver, which took four and a half hours, was an absolute nightmare. My mind started to play tricks on me. That made matters worse. Your mind has a way of doing that to your whole body. I felt lousy. I didn't want to talk, eat, or drink on the plane. My mood did not go over well with Patty. She was very angry with me and told me that I will just have to deal with it because there is nothing we can do about it. Just try to have fun on vacation. Now, that was just not going to happen. There was no way that I was going to relax and just have fun. Not realizing that I was ruining it for Patty and the kids, I just sat there brooding. Needless to say, a for a four and a half hour plane ride felt like nine hours. I just wanted to get out of that plane as fast as possible. I just wanted all of this to end quickly. I was praying to God to have this whiteness in my eye just go away. Trying to do all of this while sitting in a tightly packed space with other people was not the best place for me to be at that moment. I just wanted to be by myself in a dark room.

The plane landed at Denver International Airport. This airport is not like Philadelphia International Airport. In Philly, you get off the plane, go down to get your luggage, and then stand outside to wait for a van to pick you up to get to your car. In Denver, you have to get on a train that takes you into the terminal where your luggage is. It basically protracted my angst and anxiety. From there, you go outside and wait for a van to take you to another place to pick up your rental car. That's about a 5 to 10 minute drive. While all of this is going on, my vision is still white and I am sitting down with my hands on either side of my head in complete agony and misery. The kids and Patty are sitting on the other side of the van because they don't want to be anywhere near me. Actually, I didn't wanna be anywhere near them. Like I said before, I just wanted to be left alone. Nothing they could say would make me feel any better. When we get to the rental car place, Patty goes inside to pick out a car that she wants. The kids and I are waiting outside. Once again, I am sitting by myself on a bench with my hands on either side of my face and my elbows on my knees. The kids are standing about 10 feet away from me just talking amongst themselves. The whole situation, looking back now, must have been extremely stressful for them. What was frustrating for me at the time, was that I didn't think that they understood the magnitude of my misery at that moment. I felt like they didn't really care what was going on with me, when actually they really did but they just did not know what to say to make it feel any better Patty came out of the rental car office and we waited for our rental car to be brought to us. When it arrived, I just sat in the front seat while Patty and the kids put the luggage in the back. On the drive to our first destination, Coors Field in downtown Denver, it was a very quiet car ride. Actually, it was a very tense car ride. I just sat in the passenger seat and just looked out the side window. My vision was still white and I could barely see what we were driving by. We parked our car in the Coors Field parking lot and walked to the stadium. Our seats were in centerfield, they were called the "Rock Pile". The Colorado Rockies bullpen was just below us. Then the most amazing thing happened. All of a sudden, my vision was not white anymore. I could see clearly. I don't know if God intervened at that moment but thank God he, or she, did. The kids and Patty could tell that my mood had changed and I told them what had happened. We enjoyed the rest of the game and then drove to our house that we were renting for the week about 20 minutes outside of Denver.

The next day, we went to Rocky Mountain National Park for a hike. Now remember, I am afraid of heights. So Patty, the kids and I start to walk up this somewhat steep path to go to the top of the mountain. As we are making our way up, my knees start to get a little weak. It wasn't like we were walking on the side of the mountain. There were trees on either side of us but as we are getting higher, Patty stopped and put her hands on her knees because she was getting tired. Being the nice and thoughtful person that I am, I say to her do you want to stop? Now, the reason why I asked her if she wanted to stop was because I was getting a little afraid and I wanted to stop. Patty tells me that she is OK and we proceed upward much to my dismay. Thank God we did though. When we got to the top, there was the most amazing sight that to this day I still remember. It was called Emerald Lake. High above Emerald Lake, were snow capped mountains. It was the most peaceful place that I have ever been in my life and I wish I could go back to that time and just sit on a boulder and look at that snowcapped mountain and remember how serene I felt that day thinking back to how our vacation first started, me freaking out at the airport terminal, made this moment such a dichotomy. There was a photo that a national park worker took of all of us. With the lake behind us, and the rocky mountains behind the lake, I can still remember how we all looked on that day. I used that photo as my desktop on my computer at home. Every day when I signed on, the picture of the five of us would appear. Me wearing my black Temple University sweatshirt, Patty wearing a gray zip-up hoodie, Emily wearing a white hoodie with her name in blue spray paint across the front, Kevin wearing a plaid brown zip-up hoodie with a map in his hand, and Bryan wearing a white baseball cap with a big smile on his face. It's one of the best pictures we ever took as a family. Thinking back to that photo is bringing tears to my eyes because I realize how close I was to destroying that beautiful moment. They say that every picture tells a story, at least that's what Rod Stewart says, and that couldn't be more true. The national park worker who took that photo, had no idea what we had gone through to get to that moment. She had no idea how close I was to freaking-out in the airport. She had no idea how mad Patty was at me for being so miserable. She had no idea how disillusioned my kids were at the rental car place while I was sitting by myself on a park bench all alone. The only thought she had was what a beautiful family. They look so happy

The Retisert was doing its job and I was not encountering any inflammation in my retina. I was beginning to think that the worst was behind me. Almost every day after Patty brought me home from work, I would go outside with my boys, and occasionally Emily, and either play basketball, football or roller hockey. I can recall our standard poodle, Phoenix, sitting and watching us from the front door. We had so much fun. Me screaming like a madman like I was on the Philadelphia 76ers. Almost like I was seven years old and in my neighbor's backyard acting like I was playing for Villanova. It's funny that no matter how old you get, you still go back to when you were a little kid. For me, that little kid inside of me has never left. The neighbors probably thought I was insane. Screaming out loud whenever I made a basket. The kids would get so mad at me when

I won. I am very competitive and so are they. I was just glad that I was able to see the basket and enjoy my time with my children. Patty would occasionally come out and shoot the basketball with us. Her form was not what you would call ideal but she would make an occasional basket here or there. Then she would get mad at me teasing her and would go back inside. Such is life. Life was good again.

In 2011, my vision started to get a little worse. By this I mean that whenever I was reading a sentence on my TV screen, the far left of my screen was disappearing. So I would have to turn my head to the left to see the first word of a sentence. So for instance, if the word that I was reading was "table", I would not see the T of that word. It concerned me so I made an appointment with my doctor. Now I was seeing him about every six months at this time. Not taking any medication orally, but I was still on the pressure drops. Everything was going smoothly. When he first implanted the Retisert, he told me that the prednisone would last two years. Well at this point, it had been four years since I had the implant in my eye. When I went to see him, he told me that was the cause of my vision issues and that I needed surgery to have the implant taken out. With the Retisert taken out, my vision should improve.

My surgery was set for June 1, 2011. Patty, the kids and I had already planned on going to Washington, DC over the Memorial Day weekend. So it worked out perfectly that we could go on vacation and then I would come back and have my surgery performed. We went to Washington, DC and did all of the tourist attractions: The Smithsonian, Lincoln Memorial, Washington monument, Capitol Building and Ford Theater. The best place that we went to however, was Madame Tussaud's wax museum. They had a display of all of the presidents of the United States. They had my favorite one too, Chester A. Arthur. Now you may ask why is he my favorite president? Well, my favorite show at that time was the Simpsons. On one of the episodes, Bart plays the terminator who has a nerf gun. And his fellow classmates are presidents. I believed that Milhouse was Abe Lincoln. Anyway, Bart comes in and shoots Chester A. Arthur with a nerf gun. Hence, my favorite president. They had Richard Nixon sitting at a desk and he looked all pissed-off. They had JFK and Jackie waving to the crowd. They had Ronald Reagan sitting at a desk with a jar of jellybeans. They had Barack and Michelle Obama and of course they had my favorite, Chester A. Arthur. So while everybody is standing in front of the most famous presidents and getting their picture taken, here I am getting my picture taken with one of the most obscure ones. Did I mention that they had a wax statue of Gerald Ford and he is falling down the stairs of an airplane? Actually, he was not in that pose, but wouldn't it be hysterical if he was?

When walking, my family is usually in front of me and I am almost always the last one in a room. Bryan would be the only one that would come back and make sure that I was with them. I recall one time where I was standing in the room looking at the wax Richard Nixon and I looked around and I was the only one in the room. I was lost. Imagine that, the father was lost and not his kid. Then at that moment, Bryan came in and scolded me for not being with them. How life turns.

He was protecting me. Ironically, in 2001 when Bryan was eight years old, we were at the top of the Washington Monument waiting for an elevator. It was Patty, Kevin, Emily, Bryan and me and this one guy who looked really sweaty and nervous. Being a parent, you always look for the creepy person to protect your kids from. As the elevator doors opened, this creepy, sweaty guy knocked Bryan out of the way to get on the elevator. Did I mention that I am Italian? Did I mention that I have a temper? Did I mention that I was not on steroids at this moment? Can you imagine what I would've done if I was on steroids at that moment? Well I punched the guy in the back. We all got on the elevator and I stood in front of the guy. As the elevator doors opened, the guy tried to quickly go around me but each time he tried to go to my left I stepped to my left, and when he went to my right I went to my right. This happened for a good 50 to 60 feet on to the sidewalk. Fast forward 10 years and Bryan is 18 years old at the time. He is the one that is protecting me. He is the one that is looking out for me. That's irony at its best.

Years earlier, Patty and I went to Washington, DC without the kids and one of the coolest pictures we ever have from the trip, is of the Lincoln Memorial. What made it so unique though, was that there was a man in the foreground, who looked exactly like Abe Lincoln except he didn't have a beard. We did not notice him when we took the picture, but when we got our pictures developed, he was there. How spooky was that?

Going back to 2011, we went to a Washington Nationals and Philadelphia Phillies baseball game. We were sitting alongside the first baseline in the upper level. When we climbed the steps to our seats, that same feeling came back to me. I hate heights. I dread heights. When the game started and I was now seated, that fear went away and I got into my Philadelphia Philly game mode. This lovely, old woman sat next to me. I thought to myself, she seems like a nice lady. Well, the game began and she was loud.

I mean, loud and obnoxious. This didn't sit too well with me. She started to cheer for the Nationals very loudly, and I started to cheer for the Phillies very loudly. Did I mention that I was not on steroids at this moment? Thank God I wasn't.

After the game, we took the train back to our hotel. Patty wanted to go to the Capitol Building to listen to the Memorial Day concert and watch the fireworks afterwards. I just did not think it was that good of an idea so we stayed in our hotel room instead and watched the fireworks from our window. Kevin was 21 years old at the time and he really was not that much of a beer-drinking aficionado--this would come in about two years though. So he decided that he wanted to get a beer from the refrigerator. He opened the door, grabbed a can, and started to shake it. Then, he was about to open the tab and I yelled at him, "what are you doing?" I guess he thought he was opening up a Yoohoo. Now, Kevin works at a brewery and he would never make that same mistake again.

With another successful vacation behind us, we drove home from Washington, DC. I was looking forward to my surgery on Thursday so that my vision would be corrected. This would be my sixth eye surgery--three on my right eye and three on my left eye.

Chapter 8 – Pull Chain

On Thursday, June 1, 2011, Patty, Emily, and I went to the Pagoda Building in Bala-Cynwyd, Pennsylvania, to have my surgery performed. Emily had just completed her sophomore year in college and was home for the summer, so she went with us. In the waiting room, she was looking at her phone and not really in tune to what was going on around her. Patty was browsing through magazines while I was sitting there anxiously awaiting my name to be called.

When the nurse came out and called my name, Patty and I followed her into the pre-operating room. They placed me on a reclining chair that had wheels, and Patty gave me a kiss and wished me luck. The nurse came in and set-up an IV for me, and when my time was ready, they made the chair completely flat like a table and wheeled me into the operating room. I had done this so many times before but for some reason this time felt odd to me. I remember the first time that I had surgery performed on my right eye and the nurse would put an X above that eye to let the doctor know which one to operate on. Then each proceeding nurse that I came upon, would ask me which eye I was having surgery on. The thought came to me that somebody probably had surgery on the wrong eye, and this was the reason why they were doing this.

After the surgery was completed, they brought me into a post-operating room and I woke up to Patty's voice telling me that the surgery was a success and that the reason for my vision problems was that the implant was causing a crease on my retina. When the doctor removed the implant, he flattened out my retina and removed the crease. He said that I would make a full recovery and I should see him in four days. They patched up my left eye so that I was completely blind. That was a little freaky to me, however this was not the first time that I had a patch over my left eye and was blind after a surgery. I recall one time after I had an eye surgery, I was admitted overnight in the hospital and Patty spent the night next to me on a lounge chair. My brother-in-law came in with his brother to see me because his father was on a floor above me.

After four days, Patty drove me to see my doctor and after he took a look at my retina, he said that everything looked great. The following weekend, Patty and I, along with her friends and their spouses, went to see the movie Hangover Two. We sat all the way in the back so I really could not tell what was going on. Afterwards, we all went out for dinner and I recall looking at a TV screen and noticing that my vision seemed much better and I could see most of the screen without turning my head to the left like I had to do before the surgery. All in all it was a very enjoyable day and I was on the road to recovery.

However, on the following Tuesday, I was outside in my backyard doing some yard work and I came into our three-season room and noticed a blue plastic tub that should have been put in the basement. I should have been wearing my glasses at that time, but I went outside without wearing them. Very stupid thing for me to do and something that I would pay dearly for, for the rest of my life. I grabbed the tub and went downstairs into our basement. Our basement was not finished, but Patty and I made half the basement the kids' area to watch or play video games on TV. We had two old couches and two old chairs in front of the TV, and a foosball table and old bar behind that on one side of the basement. On the other side of the basement is where we kept storage for my in-laws and us.

The previous homeowners had left behind a warped ping-pong table. The kids and I would have a lot of fun playing ping-pong. When I was younger, we had a ping-pong table in our basement. We played so much that the tile ceiling had dents in it from swinging so hard and hitting the ceiling with our paddles. One time when we were on vacation in North Carolina, the house had a ping-pong table in the basement. Bryan and I started to play a game and when he served the ball to me, I would swing and miss because once the ball went beyond my left eye, I could not see it. I tried to keep my composure and we continued playing the game. Finally though, I lost it and threw my paddle across the floor. Bryan probably thought that I was mad at him because he was winning, but that was not the reason for my outburst. I was getting so frustrated that I was losing my vision and I could no longer do something that I loved to do since I was a little kid.

Our basement had fluorescent lights with hanging pull chains to turn the lights off and on. I carried the blue tub down the stairs and pushed aside the curtains that we had separating the two sides of the basement. I lifted up the blue tub so that it was in front of me. And without knowing, I hit the pull chain hanging from one of the fluorescent lights. This proceeded to make the pull chain like a pendulum and it swung away from me and then swung back and hit me in my left eye. That hurt like a mother. I dropped the blue tub and grabbed my left eye in pain. I found my way back to the curtain and went upstairs to the kitchen to see if I was bleeding. I had no blood on my face but when I felt my eye, my eye felt deflated. Since my vision was starting to get impaired. I called Patty at work and told her what

I had done. I was freaking-out a little bit because I knew that I had done something major to my eye. She told me that she would come home right away and I made an appointment with my doctor. When we got to his office, I could barely see anything. I remember the nurse telling me that she hoped that the doctor could do something about it. That scared the hell out of me because I already realized that I had done something very stupid, and was wondering if the damage was irreparable.

While waiting in the doctor's office with Patty, there was an older woman across the hall who was just told that she would need an injection in her eye. She was crying and I wanted so much to get off the chair and go in there and hold her hand and tell her that everything would be OK because I have had that done many times before, but I just wasn't able to get off the chair. One of the great qualities of my eye doctor was his calmness in the face of serious issues. When I told him what I had done, he very quietly and patiently told me that everything would be OK and that he would inflate air into my eye with a needle. Afterwards, I was to just go home and get some rest. I didn't believe him though. I knew that I had screwed up big-time; I was so mad at myself. How the hell could I have been so stupid and not worn my glasses downstairs? Me, of all people, should have worn glasses to protect my eyes knowing that I only had vision in one eye. I was told this so many times over the years and I still didn't listen. I didn't even listen to my ophthalmologist before all this happened. What an idiot I was. I also knew that this was different from any other procedure that I had done…whether it was the surgeries to re-attach my retina, or to remove a cataract, or to have an implant placed in my eye. All of the other procedures were not of my doing. This one was all on me

My vision never got better after that mishap. In fact, it started to get worse. With each subsequent visit to my eye doctor, the pressure in my eye was getting higher so he prescribed more pressure drops. Unlike the previous disability from work that lasted nine months, this absence would not allow me to go back to work. I was on short-term disability for three months and then on long-term disability for six months. My job would only be held for that long, and if I was not able to return to work then they would fire me.

I recall a long-term caseworker who was handling my case, crying on the phone to me when she told me that they would have to let me go. This was someone that I had never met and I had just talked to her on the phone maybe a handful of times. So here I am, almost ready to cry myself because I knew that I was going to be fired and I had to calm *her* down. Irony at its best. She was so sweet though. Sorry that I can't say the same for the human resource worker that I did know, and how she handled my situation. We had spoken a lot over the past 10 years and I had gotten to know her a little bit. When she called me and told me that they had to fire me, she couldn't have done it with less empathy. Then a week later, a box arrived at my house with all the belongings that I had on my desk. It arrived with glass items broken, and dents in anything that was tin. I was so pissed off and I gave her a call and let her know what had happened. She told me to give her a dollar amount of how much my belongings had cost. I called her back and told her $200, and then she proceeded to tell me that they could only pay me $100 for my belongings. I was a month shy of working at my job for 24 years…24 years and I get $100 for my belongings? How shitty is that?

Here I was, 47 years old and on Social Security Disability. I was angry. I was depressed. I was frustrated. I was resentful. I went into a protective shell from the world. This was the beginning of a long and winding road to the bottom. It had been over 10 years since I first noticed the whiteness in my right eye while painting the kitchen walls and the vaulted ceiling. At that moment, I didn't think that life could get any worse. Boy was I wrong.

In July, Patty and I went over to celebrate my great niece's second birthday. Once again, I didn't want to be there. I only wanted to be at home. It was a beautiful day and my niece had picnic tables in her backyard for everyone to sit and eat. My sister had just come home from a vacation to Germany and was showing everyone pictures of her trip. I was sitting at an adjacent table to her, and wasn't speaking. She started the conversation off by saying that she had a great time in Germany. I slowly looked at her and said, "that's nice". I didn't care. I really didn't care about anything but myself.

We stayed until they sang happy birthday to my great niece and then we left. I couldn't believe that my sister had brought up her trip to Germany, but didn't ask how I was doing. In hindsight, I was being very selfish. I didn't want anyone to have any happiness in their lives if I wasn't happy. I was very bitter. It also didn't help matters that I could not see the photos of her trip.

The rest of the summer, while Patty was working, I stayed in bed all day. I got up in the morning to eat breakfast with her and then went back to bed until noon. When I got out of bed, I would go down and eat lunch. My kids would be sitting on the couch and I wouldn't even say anything to them, and they wouldn't say anything to me. I felt so miserable and alone. They didn't know what to say to me. It must have been really hard for them to see their father like that. I used to be such a fun person to be around, and now I wasn't. It was like walking on egg shells around me. Who knew when I would explode? After I ate lunch, I would go back upstairs and get into bed. It was like that every day for the rest of the summer.

Chapter 9 - Goodbye Mom

There is a picture of my mom where she was standing on the beach somewhere down south. She was in a plain dress and was looking out at the ocean. More than likely, my dad took that picture. She was very young, probably in her mid to late 20s. She was a very beautiful woman. I could understand why my dad married her. She looked so elegant on that beach, almost like Princess Grace. This was before she had children. She looked so peaceful. Of course, peace was not in the cards for her future because she had six children and we were a wild bunch.

My mom was never really healthy her whole life. She had to deal with COPD from the second-hand smoke she had to breathe from my grandfather and his constant smoking. She also did not have a very strong heart. Now add to that having six children with one of them being disabled--this caused a lot of stress on her body. It did not stop her from going on vacations with our family down the shore, and bossing everybody around. It never stopped her from doing what she loved the most, sewing. It never stopped her from going to the casinos, either in Atlantic City or Las Vegas, and sitting at her favorite slot machine and dropping quarter after quarter. It didn't stop her from chasing me around our kitchen table after I said a curse word, or yelling at my sisters and brother to catch me so that she could put Ivory dishwashing liquid in my mouth.

There is an old saying, that goes, "when they made you, they broke the mold". That could not resonate more when describing my mom. She was the oldest of seven. She got married when she was 24 and had her first child when she was 26. Like I said before, she had five children in seven years including having two children in one calendar year... only separated by 11 months. They call that Irish twins. Then six years later came me. The story goes in my family, that when my mom would take in foster children, my siblings would get very close to them. When it was time for the foster child to leave, my siblings would be very upset. So my mom decided that she wanted to have another child. I think this is complete bullshit. This is how I think everything went down. I'm an "oops". Yup. Do you really believe that my dad wanted to have a sixth child? Do you really believe that my mom wanted to have a sixth child? No way in hell. They were done with children. They had their hands full with five children, they didn't want another one running around the house and driving them crazy like my five siblings did at that time.

I was born in 1963, when my mom was 38 and my dad was 43. I'm 57 right now and I can't imagine having a 14-year-old child driving me nuts. I mean I get tired just getting out of bed after sleeping for eight hours. Imagine trying to deal with a teenager and all of the issues that come with that? No way! Sorry, Patty, it's not gonna happen. So that's why I say I was an "oops". My dad probably came home from work really tired and just was not thinking straight. That's my story and I'm sticking to it.

When Patty was pregnant with Bryan, we went over to the old Cape Cod house for Christmas. It was 1992 and everybody was sitting in the basement. The tile floor, black and white checkered couch, and the wood-paneled walls. It never changed over the years. We have a video of my mom opening up a box that we gave to her telling her that her Christmas present was an eighth grandchild. Now, my mom always showed such expression on her face. When she was confused, her eyebrows would raise up. So she was reading the card that we have in this box and up go those eyebrows. She started reading the note that we put in there about having an eighth grandchild and you could see that just for a split second she was not understanding any of it. Then the lightbulb went off in her head and she screamed. My mom was always a loud person, whether she was mad or happy. At this moment, she was happy. And everybody knew it.

My mom was not always the most tactful person though. There was no filter between her brain and her mouth and that sometimes got her in trouble. On Halloween, my mom would have the trick-or-treaters come into our living room. They had to either do a trick or say something like a joke to get their treat. Now the treat wasn't worth what she was asking these poor trick-or-treaters to do. It was probably an apple or something stupid like that. Year after year though, these trick-or-treaters came into our living room to entertain my mom. One year, after my mom invited a trick-or-treater into our living room, and asked him to do a trick for his treat, the kid said out loud to his friend, "I knew this was the house"!

My mom had so many idiosyncrasies to mention, but I can't fit them all into this book.

My mom had a lot of style, but you would never know it by the clothes that she bought for me. There is a picture of me standing next to my dad at my sister's wedding, and we both look ridiculous. My mom also bought clothes for my dad and in that picture he looks like a pimp and I look like my jacket was caked in glue and Rip Taylor came and threw confetti up in the air and I ran through it. My dad and I are both laughing and it is probably because I saw his suit and laughed, and he saw my suit and laughed. There was this other photo with our whole family standing in front of trees. A real nice photo of all of us but the one thing that stands out is my suit looks like I escaped from a prison. The suit had lines going straight down and straight across. My dad and I are standing behind my mom, who is seated, and we both have our hand on her shoulder. We probably wanted to choke her for the clothes that she bought for us. We both were dressed by my mom like we were orphans in the movie Oliver. One time my mom bought me two button-down long sleeve shirts from the thrift store. One was blue-and-white checkered and the other one was red-and-white checkered. I wore the red-and-white checkered shirt to high school one day and while sitting at the lunch table, one of my friends said my shirt looked like a picnic tablecloth. That was the last time I ever wore that shirt, and I never allowed my mom to buy me any more clothes. As for my dad, he was tortured for the rest of his life.

When my mom cleaned the house, she really cleaned the house. I had a bookshelf in my bedroom and had Sports Illustrated magazines in chronological order. One day when I came home from school, there was a Playboy magazine on my bed. I thought that I could hide that magazine amongst my Sports Illustrated magazines, but "Sherlock Holmes" found it! Why was she looking through my Sports Illustrated magazines? I have no idea. Maybe my brother ratted me out.

My mother should have been a funeral critic for the Philadelphia Inquirer because she never went to a funeral without commenting on it. It was never sad enough for her liking. She would come home from a funeral and say that they weren't crying enough. It was like my mom was Steven Spielberg and she was writing down director notes so she could tell the family afterwards that they could do better. She was crazy like that. My good friend Matt, passed away at the age of 25 from meningitis. It was heartbreaking for me and Patty because he was such a great kid. My mother had never met him before, but she wanted to go to his funeral. I pleaded with her not to do so. Patty and I went to St Anastasia's Church for his mass. While we are sitting in the pew, guess who shows up? Yup! Here comes my mom, dressed to the nines by the way, sitting in a pew about 10 rows in front of us. Afterwards, when Patty and I get home, my mother says that she did not think that the family was sad enough. I say to her, who asked you to go? That was my mom.

Everybody has issues with their mother when they are growing up. It wasn't any different for me. My mom could get on my nerves and I could get on her nerves. As my mom started to age though, I started to appreciate her much more. Having kids of my own, I understood how difficult it was to raise your children. I understood the financial burdens that are placed on a parent, and the walking of the fine line between discipline and love.

Here's where it's going to get tough for me to talk about. Reminiscing about your parents is always a difficult thing to do without getting emotional. My mom and dad were both Italian and both had tempers. My dad cursed a lot and my mom never did. She let my dad have it every time he cursed and my dad let her have it every time she got mad at him for cursing…not a good mix when they were living together and everyone was out of the house. It seemed like the only time they were happy and smiling was when the whole family was back at that old Cape Cod house for the holidays. It's sad to think that their once loud-and-crazy family was gone and now they were left them with a very quiet home and themselves to deal with.

As my mom got older, her issues with COPD and her heart started to manifest much more frequently, and it slowed her down. I remember one time my mom telling me that she was out of breath all the time and I told her to just go outside and walk down to the mailbox and back to the home every day for some little exercise. Even that was too difficult for her to do and she also was afraid that she would fall down. Throughout all of this though, I never really heard her complain. I have to give her a lot of credit for that, because most people would. That was their generation though, they never complained because they were happy with what they had and didn't bitch about what they didn't have.

When it got too difficult for my mom to be at home, we all looked around for a good place for her to live. We finally decided on a place that was an hour and a half away from Patty and me. She moved into an assisted-living apartment and was so happy. It was the first time in her life that she had lived alone and she was reveling in the sanctity of a quiet place. That did not stop her from speaking without thinking. One time when Patty and I were visiting her, she asked Patty to grab a scissor and cut a hair that was growing above her lip. Yup. Patty had to cut a hair on her mother-in-law's lip. That was my mom.

As my mom's health deteriorated, so did my vision. I had always been close with my siblings, but with my mom and dad being placed in an assisted-living center, we started to grow apart. Patty's mom was dealing with health issues of her own, and Patty and the kids had to care for her. With me not driving, I could not go and see my mom and dad as much as I would have liked to do. I wasn't able to go over there and help them with any of their needs. I felt useless, worthless, and hopeless. Whenever I got a call from one of my sisters or brother, telling me what was going on with my mom or dad, I would get resentful. Resentful because I was not able to help them out.

I did call my mom and dad every week to see how they were doing, but to me it just wasn't the same as being there, holding my mom's hand and telling her that everything would be OK. So I got angry at my siblings. I never actually came out and told them that I was mad, but I was mad. Actually, I was mad at everybody. Mostly, I was mad at myself. Mad at myself because I couldn't do what they were doing, and I was jealous. Also, with my mother-in-law going through her health issues, I wasn't able to go over and see my mom and dad as much as I would've liked to. Asking Patty to drive me to see my mom and dad once a month was hard enough because of how far away they lived. But then include Patty having to deal with her mother's health issues was just too much to ask of her. I would tell my mom and dad how bad I felt, and they would say that just me calling them was good enough. Good enough was not good enough for me though.

In November 2011, my mom and dad's beautiful, old Cape Cod home was put up for sale. My sisters and brother took care of cleaning-up the house and getting any repairs fixed. I was not really involved because I couldn't help out that much due to my disability and how far away I lived--not to mention Patty dealing with her mother. This made me feel like shit. During this time, my sisters and brother got much closer. They were in the same boat and I was in the dinghy, so to speak. I had no idea what they were going through and they had no idea what I was going through. I really wished that I could have switched places with them.

In January, 2012, the old Cape Cod house was sold and we all went back to the home for one last walk-through. I went upstairs into my old bedroom by myself and just cried. All my frustration, resentment, anger, and jealousy came to the surface. I didn't want to leave that room. I wanted to sit on the floor and never leave.

When it was time to go, I walked to our car in the driveway and leaned up against it. My sisters and brother came out of the house at the same time and hugged each other and cried. I watched them and thought about going over to join them but decided not to. They did all the work. I have done nothing. At that moment, I felt so alone. I felt like I was not a part of the family. All of this was going on just as I was losing my job and slowly losing my vision. Here I'm thinking, I'm going to lose my family.

As my mother's condition worsened, she was moved to the skilled-nursing unit of the center. In October, 2011, the staff at the nursing home told us that my mom was not going to get any better and that they would place her in hospice care. When my mother was told that, it was one of the few times that I had ever seen her cry. She was a tough lady but this was just too tough for her to handle. She had been through a lot in her life while dealing with her health issues and handling a mentally-impaired child.

I was sitting in my family room watching TV when my sister called me on my cell phone. When I answered, all my siblings were on the phone as well. My sister waited for everybody to get on the phone at the same time so that she could tell the news to us. My mom did not have much time to live. Maybe a week or two weeks. This was on Friday, December 2, 2011. I was numb. Nothing can prepare you for this. You always think that your parents are invincible and will always be there. It's not until you get older that you realize that they are vulnerable.

Sunday, December 4, 2011, Patty, Kevin, Emily and I went to visit my mom and dad in the nursing home. My mom and dad looked so happy. They always looked happy whenever we came over to see them at the house. This was no different, but it really was different. My mom was dying but she looked so happy. I was confused. My mother was a very religious woman. She always prayed the rosary while lying in bed. Maybe she had come to terms with all of this and her mortality. I don't know because I didn't ask her.

It was such a lovely visit. We talked and laughed just like we always did. I asked my mom about when she was younger did she date a lot. My mom said that she would go out on dates on the premise that her date would buy her chocolate ice cream. Emily laughed so hard. I think Emily appreciated my mom much more as she got older. She saw that my mom was really funny and not a strict Italian woman.

When it was time to go, we wheeled my mom and dad back to their rooms. We passed by a room that had a scale and my mom wanted to weigh herself. Patty wheeled her on the scale and when my mom read the reading she asked Patty to go over to the nurse to let her know. Amazing. My mom is weighing herself knowing that she will soon be in heaven. I guess she wanted to look good for God. Who knows. When we approach the nurse however, the nurse is a complete ass to my mom. Giving her such an attitude. I really wish that I could go back in time and curse that nurse out. I would have told her, "How dare you treat my mother like that! This is a woman that will soon be gone from us. You were treating her like dirt. Why don't you go home and leave her alone. Would you treat your mother like that?" I didn't though because I was just too sad.

We bring my dad to his room and we all say goodbye and then we bring my mother to her room and help her into bed. My mother was knitting a baby cap for infants that were born prematurely. I was so impressed. She was showing Patty, Kevin, and Emily her craftsmanship and I was standing about 10 feet away trying to compose myself. I wanted to be strong for her. When it was time for us to go, Kevin and Emily gave my mom a hug and a kiss and told her that they loved her and she told them that she loved them too. Then it was Patty's turn and my mom told Patty that she was a great daughter-in-law. I'm thinking to myself, yeah, she damn right is a good daughter-in-law. What daughter-in-law would cut a hair above their mother-in-law's lip? Only my mom however would ask her daughter-in-law to do that. Finally, it was my turn to say goodbye. I walked over to the left side of my mom's bed and leaning down, grabbed her hand and gave her a kiss. I told her that I loved her and she told me that I was a faithful son. Wow! That hit me hard. Here I was hating myself for not doing more to help my mom and dad, and my mother realized it. It was like she was telling me, don't worry about it son, I know you did your best.

On Wednesday night, my sister called me up and said that my mom took a turn for the worse that she was in a coma. Kevin drove me to the nursing home on Thursday, December 8 and we went into my mom's room. My sister was in the room with my mom and she was talking very quietly to her. When my sister noticed us, she told us to go out into the hall. She sat us down on the bench and told us that the nurse had come in and told her that my mother probably would not make it through the weekend. The nurse was wrong however because my mom didn't make it through that day. She passed away at 7:30 PM with all her family around her. I was sitting off to my mom's right, holding her right hand when she passed. I didn't know that she had passed, because for the first time in what seems like ages, I felt peaceful. It was almost like my mom's strength had left her and went into me. Sounds crazy but I really believe that's what happened.

My mom with buried on December 16, 2011, in Calvary Cemetery in West Conshohocken, Pennsylvania. Standing in the receiving line was surreal for me. That's the first time that I ever had to do that. I always was the one that was going through the receiving line telling someone who had lost a loved one that I was sorry. Now this was happening to me and it was really weird. I was a pallbearer and when I went to grab the casket I could not find the handle. My niece's husband helped me out with that and we walked the casket into the church. My sister and niece both gave beautiful eulogies. Afterwards, we went to a local restaurant for a luncheon. I was seated at a table with my siblings and my father. I felt really uncomfortable because I still was not on the best of terms with them. When they placed the meal in front of me, I didn't even want to eat. I was numb. My sister stood up and thanked everyone for coming but I said nothing. Better that I didn't because I probably would have broken down. Broken down because I had lost my mother and broken down because I was so heartbroken about my lost vision. Sounds really selfish doesn't it? That's how I was feeling at the time though. I can't tell you anything other than the truth.

On Christmas 2011, we went to my sister's house. It felt kind of hollow and shallow. I was in no mood for Christmas. On Christmas morning before we went over to my sister's, I was so emotional. Every time that my wife or children opened up a gift, tears would roll down my cheeks. I couldn't help it.

My sister's house had stairs that went from her kitchen up to her bedroom. I sat on the stairs looking around at everybody. I wanted to be alone. I didn't want to be there. It wasn't the same. My dad was there and I don't think he looked very happy either. Everybody was going through the motions though. I wasn't any different than anybody else. This was the beginning of a new normal in my life. It wasn't going to be easy, but then again life isn't easy.

For whatever reason, I like songs that are depressing. Maybe it matches my pessimistic outlook on life. That's why I love the Counting Crows so much. Most of their songs appeal to me. So at this time in my life, I put pen to paper and wrote down how I was feeling after my mothers passing. At the luncheon after my mom's burial, we were served meat and potatoes. I did not have much of an appetite at that time. The first lyric that I wrote was in reference to how I felt. After that, the lyrics flowed into symmetry and visual effects that I would never see again in my future.

I didn't feel anything about anything or anyone the days following my mom's passing.in subsequent months and years, those feelings would be more embellished. The following is a lyric that I wrote and then my daughter provided music and then Bryan added his voice to complete the song. It is called numb. That's how I felt. No feelings at all. I didn't care about anything. All I did was care about myself. Wallowing in my self-pity. Wondering if I would ever be happy again.

Numb
By Dennis Savini

[verse 1]
I have a plate before me
Filled with potatoes and meat
I'm feeling so hungry
But I don't want to eat
I' came home to your note
Saying you had enough
You left your hat and coat
And took the rest of your stuff

[chorus]
I'm feeling numb
About what's been done
Feeling this numb
Sure isn't fun
I might succumb
To feeling numb

[verse 2]
I've lost all emotion
Forgotten how to grieve
No waves in my ocean

There's no salt in my sea
When you walked out the door
Storm clouds came rolling in
The rain began to poor
My whole world was flood'n

[chorus]
I'm feeling numb
About what's been done
Feeling this numb
Sure isn't fun
I might succumb
To feeling numb

[bridge]
Maybe one day I'll talk
Maybe one day I'll listen
Take my heart out of the box
Cutting away the ribbons
Until then…

[verse 3]
The sun won't shine as bright
The sky won't be as blue
No moon comes out at night
No stars will come in view
I will not smell the grass
I will not feel the breeze
I will not hear the brass
I will not see the trees.

[chorus]
I'm feeling numb

Chapter 10 - Shingles

In 2012, I was out of work and at home by myself all day. At this point, Patty was at work, Kevin was commuting to college, and Emily and Bryan were living on campus at their respective colleges. I would do chores around the home during the day and mostly watch TV and sulk. I was seeing my regular eye doctor, but one time he could not make my appointment so I saw his associate. This guy was a team doctor for one of the Philadelphia major-league sports. He was the opposite of my regular doctor when it came to bedside manners. He made Dr. No Bedside Manners look like a priest in comparison. I had made an appointment because I was getting a headache over my left eye and I felt like my pressure was up. It was never good to have high pressure in your eye because it could lead to glaucoma and other issues. My eye doctor always told me that whenever I felt uncomfortable, to make an appointment any time--not to wait. So this is what I did. Unfortunately, like I said before, he was not there to see me so I had to see this idiot. This idiot had never seen me before and when he came into the room I felt uncomfortable. It seemed to me like he had a cold because his nose sounded stuffed up. If I could describe him, he had thinning hair and was normal height. Other than the fact that he was a complete asshole, there wasn't really much else to describe. As soon as he started to talk, I knew I was in trouble. With an attitude, he asked me why I came for an appointment. I told him why and he checked my pressure. Like I knew, it was elevated. The asshole then said to me that I shouldn't see a glaucoma specialist when I brought it up to him. Dr. Idiot said that the glaucoma specialist would handle my elevated pressure just like they were doing--prescribing pressure drops. All of this said to me with an attitude. My mental state was fragile at that time and I got pissed-off at him. Rightfully so. No doctor should talk to any patient like that.

Kevin was with me at the appointment and he sat there listening to the conversation. Kevin is not one for confrontation. I, on the other hand, thrive on confrontations. I wasn't about to let this shithead get the best of me. Unfortunately, he did get the best of me when we had the following discussion. When I asked him his opinion on my vision, he said that it would never get any better. This was the opposite of what my regular doctor had said. My regular doctor was an optimist and this doctor was a realist. When I told him what my regular doctor had told me, he said "I guess he is playing good cop and I am playing bad cop". Nice! The first time I had seen this fucking doctor and he breaks my heart. He broke my heart so coldly too.

On the way home I was so upset. I was not expecting that answer. Kevin and I weren't on the best of terms at that time. Well, actually the kids and I were not on speaking terms at that time. I was miserable and depressed and angry and any other emotion you want to add. Patty and the kids had seen my emotional decline, not to mention they had to deal with my mother-in-law's mental decline. So I really don't believe that Kevin heard what the doctor had told me, or knew how devastating it was to me. He was probably on his phone at the time and didn't realize the magnitude of the situation. As we are driving home, Kevin asked me if I wanted to get lunch. That was the last thing in the world that I wanted to get. I didn't want to eat. My stomach was so upset. I wanted to cry but I didn't want to cry in front of Kevin. I did my crying when I was alone.

In July, 2012, once again I noticed an irregularity in my vision. I was on hyper alert for any visual decrease. I was starting to see double. When I called to make an appointment, however, my regular doctor was in Delaware so I had to see Dr. Idiot instead. I was not happy about this. I was in no mood for his bullshit.

When he came into the office, I was prepared for him. I tensed-up and when he asked me what the problem was, I told him the problem but with an attitude. He was not going to get the best of me this time. I was going to let him know that you were not gonna fuck with me. Maybe you can fuck around with older patients because they are older and are vulnerable, but you ain't gonna pull that shit over me again. When he took a look at my eye, his whole demeanor softened. He called my regular doctor and told him that I was having issues and he wanted to know if he could give me another Kenalog injection. He was not sure what the problem was, but he told my doctor that the inside of my eye was lit up. Not good news. Been down this road before. I'm thinking to myself, what now?

Before when I got eye injections, they would clamp my upper and lower eyelids apart. Dr. Idiot didn't do that. Dr Idiot just told me to look at my nose, and without clamps, put an injection into my eye. My eye reacted differently than it ever did to a Kenalog injection. I knew that something was wrong right away.

The doctor also prescribed me medication since he was not sure what the problem was. I made an appointment at the front desk to see my regular doctor at Wills Eye Hospital in a week.

When I went into see my regular doctor a week later, he told me that I had shingles in my eye. Usually, shingles will appear on the skin if you had chickenpox in the past. Of course with me, the shingles appeared in my eye. It was like my eye was a magnet for bad news. He was much more concerned and understanding of my emotions. He truly did feel bad for me. He was just as frustrated as I was because he just could not get a handle on the situation. We were both going through this together. You could see it in his eyes. He was a professional all the way.

After the visit with my regular doctor, Patty and I went to the Wells Fargo Center in Philadelphia to see Aerosmith and Cheap Trick. The place was packed and Steven Tyler did not disappoint. There was a ramp that led from the main stage out to center court where there was a little stage. At the little stage was a piano and Steven Tyler played Dream On. It was awesome. The only thing that would have made the night perfect, was if I could see what was going on. A shade started to develop in the upper quadrant of my eye. It was almost like a windshield that had a tinted portion of it down to the visor. On top of that shade was a blinking red light in my central vision. My doctor told me that the medication that was injected into my eye was building-up on the bottom portion of my eye. When you look out, what you see on the top of your eye is actually on the bottom of your eye because your vision is flipped upside down. Got all that? Good! I didn't believe that was the case. I believed that something was wrong. What I have learned through this whole process by now, is that you know your body better than anybody else--no matter if this doctor is a specialist in his field. Never, ever did I go by what a doctor said. I was my own best advocate. Doctors make mistakes too.

When I went back to my doctor, the shade in my eyes started to come in from my nose to my central vision. I felt like the world was closing in on me. My doctor then told me that it was not the medication that was causing the issue, which I had already known before, and that the darkness was due to the damage done to my retina and optic nerve by the shingles. This time, I braced myself for the bad news. I knew it was bad. I had brought up the issue of my right eye at that appointment. I asked him what was the possibility of me getting vision back in my right eye since that's what he told me could possibly happen when I saw him almost 10 years ago. He said that he never told me that I would get sight back in my right eye, and that it was a dead eye. When Patty and I questioned him on that, he held steadfast to his comment that he never said that I would get vision back in that right eye. He had lied to us. For me, that was it. When he lied to me, my trust in him had died.

After I was diagnosed with shingles, I started to notice a small white light in my central vision. It looked like what a hurricane would look like on a map. Slowly it would get larger and larger until it took up my whole vision. My eye would then be white for 24 hours. It drove me crazy. I went to see a neurological ophthalmologist about this issue and he told me that there really was nothing that he could do about it. My optic nerve was damaged and my brain was trying to send signals through my optic nerve but since it was so messed up, it was misfiring. That was the cause of the whiteness. Since I was having a lot of difficulty dealing with this whiteness, Patty took me to center city Philadelphia to visit a store for the blind to purchase sunglasses. These glasses protected 99% of the light that was coming in through the glasses.

When I was in the car with Patty, I sat in the backseat and put a blanket over my head. I was trying everything to protect the whiteness coming into my vision. Nothing worked. It was horrible. With the whiteness over my whole eyes, I was starting to get headaches. The whiteness in my eye was so powerful that it was like I was looking into the head lights of a tractor trailer. The next day when I woke up, the whiteness was gone and my vision was back to normal, or what you would call normal for me.

I would sit at the dinner table with my sunglasses on because the lights in the kitchen were bothering my eyesight. My vision was becoming very sensitive to light. It got so bad, that Patty and I would eat dinner with the kitchen lights off and candles lit. Not what you would call candle light dining in its purest definition. Patty tried everything to make me comfortable, but I was just so miserable.

One morning when I woke up, what I had been dreaming about was in my vision. It was the strangest thing. For instance, if I was dreaming about a person, when I woke-up that person was in my vision. It was really freaky. It wasn't a still shot of that person, that person was moving. If I was dreaming about a horse running, when I woke up the horse was running in my vision. I thought I was going insane. In order to clear the image, I would have to shake my head with my eyes open for about ten minutes.

My neurological ophthalmologist told me that this issue was called Charles Bonnet syndrome. It was another side effect of having a damaged optic nerve. Once again, I asked him if there was anything that he could do about the whiteness in my vision, hoping that he could come up with something. He told me that I could take some medication but these medications also had side effects. One of the medications he mentioned, was for people who are schizophrenic. No thank you. Who knows, maybe I was schizophrenic..

Each time I visited him, I kept pressing him to come up with some answers for my problem. He was a really nice guy and he kept on trying. He then told me to go to Wills Eye Hospital and to get my eyes checked out again by having an MRI of my brain. This procedure would be twofold, one to quell any doubts to Patty that I had a brain, and the other one was to see if there were any other issues causing this problem. When the MRI was completed, the radiologist at the hospital thought that she saw some swelling in my optic nerve. She thought that this could be the problem. Patty and I were so relieved and excited for the possibility of coming up with a solution to my problem. It seemed like there was finally hope. I was admitted overnight and put on an IV that would pump prednisone into my body for 24 hours. The thought process was that the prednisone would alleviate the swelling in my eye and correct the issue.

I went to bed with such high aspirations and when I woke up I noticed that the eye was still the same. When my doctor came in to see me, he told me that the prednisone wasn't working and that more than likely there was no swelling in my optic nerve. At least he had tried. He gave it his all. He wanted me to stay at least two more days to continue the treatment. Patty and Kevin came to visit me and Patty helped cut my food and helped me to eat. By this time, the shade in my eye was coming from not only the top and right side of my eye, but the left side as well. This left me with vision in the bottom left side of my eye, and even that wasn't great. When Patty and Kevin left, I got so emotional. I had gone from such a high to such a low in 24 hours. I had hope and then I had lost that hope. The next day, a male nurse came in and brought my food. I asked him if he could cut it up for me and he obliged. He was so nice. I felt so weak and useless. Having somebody cut up my food and I was only 48 years old. It had been 14 months since I had surgery to remove the implant and then walked into a pull chain which deflated my eye. I was close to hitting rock-bottom.

When I was released from the hospital, my family and I went to the cemetery where my mother was buried. They had finally placed a tombstone at her gravesite. With my siblings, their spouses, and their children at the gravesite, we all gathered around. Next to my mother and father's plot, was my uncle and aunt's plot. My aunt had died about 10 years prior and their son had died about 15 years ago. It was a solemn event. The skies were cloudy and when I arrived at the gravesite, the sun shone through an opening in the clouds and illuminated my mother's tombstone. It was amazing. The problem was that I could not read the engraving on the tombstone. I was getting emotional and was trying my best to keep it inside. My sister grabbed my finger and placed it over the engraving so I could feel the letters. Just then, tears started rolling down my cheek. I was wearing my sunglasses at the time, so I tried my best to hide the tears by wiping them off my cheeks, but everybody noticed. The absolute grief and guilt that I had for not being able to help my siblings care for my mother, came to the surface once again.

I felt like I was slowly falling into a well and the rope was getting harder for me to hold onto.

My two sisters, brother and I went to see a medium. Now I know a lot of people don't believe in mediums but we made an appointment to see one in August. We were all feeling a lot of grief since the passing of my mother and I guess we were looking for some signal from her to tell us that she was OK and that we would be OK. The medium had a small office and we sat in chairs in front of her. She was a very nice woman and made us all feel at ease. My vision at that time was almost nonexistent and I was wearing my sunglasses because the light in her office was affecting my eyes.

My sister was recording the session on her phone. I am glad that she did because I really was not listening to what the medium was saying. I was in a fog. I was there but I wasn't there mentally. I didn't know if the medium was talking to me, so my sisters would tell me "she's talking to you, Dennis". As we had hoped, my mother came through and talked to each one of us. I had never been to a medium before and was skeptical but it really did seem like the medium was talking to my mother. She knew my mother's name, Catherine, and all of her idiosyncrasies.

Afterword, we left the room and walked out into the parking lot. Patty had driven me so she was in the waiting room while we were having our session. We said goodbye to everyone and then Patty and I got into our car and left the parking lot. I just lost it in the car. I started to cry not so much that my mother had come through, but that my vision was so bad that I was scared to death of going blind. Just then, my sister ran to our car as we were driving by because she had forgotten to give us an envelope with my mother's photos in it. She noticed me crying and tried to comfort me. She thought that I was emotional from the session, but that was not the reason.

I did not tell her the real reason because I knew that she was emotional as well.

My sister gave us a CD of the session that she had burned from her phone. I listened to it and noticed things the medium had said that I did not hear her say before. My mother was talking to me and she was saying that I was giving up. She told me that I was stronger than I thought I was and to keep on fighting. I was giving up. She knew I was giving up. The hard thing though, was that I didn't think I was strong enough to fight. I was listening to the CD in my family room while sitting in the dark. At that time, whenever I was in a room, I sat in the dark. My eyes were so sensitive to the light. It was almost like I was blind already. Sitting in a room with no lights. Anything made me cry. I was so emotional. I listened to that CD over and over and over again, trying to find some peace and inner strength.

In September, Patty and I were going to see Bruce Springsteen and the E St. Band at Citizens Bank Park in Philadelphia. The concert was over the Labor Day weekend and we had bought those tickets a while ago. This was before the episode with shingles and I was really looking forward to seeing him. As the concert neared, I started to get cold feet. At that time in my life, I just wanted to be home all of the time. That was my safe place. The week of the concert, I told Patty about my reservations of going to the concert and asked her if her friend would go in my place. If you know how much I love Bruce Springsteen and the E St. Band, you would know that I was in a bad place. The day of the concert, Patty kept on asking me if I was sure about not going. I told her yes. I really wanted to go though. I wanted to get off the couch, put my shoes on and go to see him, but I was just broken inside. Afraid of going out in public like a blind man. Ashamed for who I was becoming.

When Patty left to go to the concert, I laid down on the couch in the dark in my family room and just cried for three hours. I was so angry at myself for not going.

There is a song by Green Day, called Wake Me Up When September Ends. It is such a good song. Billie Joe Armstrong wrote it about his father passing in September and how he felt each time the month of September rolled in. September, 2012, was one of those months for me. Every time I hear that song I think of my dad.

Chapter 11- Goodbye Dad

My dad was the third of five sons born to Frank and Annacelia. He played most sports in high school-- including basketball when they shot the ball underhand, and football when they wore leather helmets.

He was from the greatest generation and served as a marine during World War II, receiving shrapnel wounds in his shoulder and hand during the battle of Iwo Jima. He would tease his grandchildren by telling them that he had the shrapnel removed from his body, and then he would come into the living room with nuts and bolts inside a mason jar. He got a kick out of their reaction.

The night that my mom met my dad, she was with her sister. My dad told my mom to get into the front seat with him, patting the seat next to him. My mom obliged, she probably thought she was going to get chocolate ice cream out of the deal, and got into the car with her sister sitting against the passenger door. When my dad asked my mom what her name was, she said "Mabel". Really, mom? You couldn't think of something better than Mabel? Anyway, they dated for three years and when my dad was 30, my mom's dad pulled him aside and asked him what his intentions were with my mother. Basically, my granddad was telling my dad, "when are you going to marry my daughter?" Shit or get off of the pot, Woody.

My dad was five feet nine and probably weighed no more than 160 pounds. To me though, he was much larger in stature. He was like Superman without the cape. Instead he wore a white V-neck undershirt with the sleeves cut off. Add to that a red and white bandana that he tied around his neck and a baseball cap that he wore with the brim just above his eyes. That was my dad's look whether it would be in our backyard cutting the grass or doing work on the golf course where he was the head greenskeeper.

My dad had this stride that meant all business. He was always on the move no matter what he was doing. He never slowed down. He also had the largest hands of any man I ever met. They were the size of a baseball glove. No matter how hot or humid it got, he would still wear that ratty undershirt and a pair of Dickies. My father had what you would call the epitome of a farmer's tan. His hands, arms, and the portion of his skin not covered by that V-neck undershirt, were dark brown. He never wore shorts around the house or at work. I saw him in a pair of shorts maybe a handful of times during my lifetime. As dark as his arms were though, his legs were white as a ghost. Those legs never saw the sun. I bet the sun laughed at his legs. My dad rarely went on vacation with our family. He was always working. However, in 1975 when I was 12 years old, my mom, dad, sister, brother-in-law, and I went to Disney World. We went to River Country for the day, and that's when I saw my dad in a tan bathing suit with those white, ghostly legs. Thank God the lifeguard was wearing sunglasses, because he probably would have fallen from his post into the water. We all prepared to go on this waterslide. I went first, followed by my sister and brother-in-law. We were holding onto the side of the slide waiting for my mom and dad to come down. My mom appeared and then my dad with white legs hanging off the side of the inner tube and his hair up in the air. Here came Superman without a cape, sliding down in an inner tube and his body was all wet. You see, Superman had problems getting on his inner tube. Dumb ass.

That was the first time that I really saw my dad having fun and being relaxed. For the most part, he usually was not in the best of moods and was tired most of the time. His job was grueling. He would get up at 3 AM to go to work and then come home around 5 PM. He did this every Monday through Friday and then on the weekends he would get up at 3 AM and work until noon. He didn't really have much time for relaxation or time to spend with me. As a young kid, I didn't understand that. Going to Disney World though, I saw a side of my father that I had never seen before. Also, it was unusual to see my mom and dad together, and not yelling at one another. They were having such a great time, and it was a lot of fun to see.

When my dad got home from work, my mom would tell him if I had been bad, and he would call me over and have me lay across his lap to get strapped. My dad was like Clint Eastwood with that belt. If you were around him and you pissed him off, that belt would come off his pants so quick it was amazing. My dad had steely blue eyes and when you pissed him off, he would just give you a look. It scared the living shit out of me. It sent chills down my spine. I learned quickly not to piss him off so I wouldn't get the Clint Eastwood treatment with that strap and the steely-eyed look.

In the winter, he would put chains on the tires of that old Caprice Classic and then attach a snowplow to his old Ford F150 truck. He would get up early in the morning when there was a winter storm and plow not only our driveway but our street. I'm sure that this pissed-off all our neighbors because they were hoping that they would not have to go to work. They would look out their window at night time and see the snow falling and think to themselves, great, I won't be able to get out of our neighborhood tomorrow morning. Then the next morning they would wake up, and they would see my dad plowing the street and get all pissed-off at him. This didn't happen, but this is what I think was going on in their minds. Stupid Woody.

Almost every day when he came home from his stressful job, my dad would either make a manhattan or a whiskey sour. He would sometimes have a manhatten in a mason jar which he kept in a sock in his truck, just in case he couldn't wait until he got home. I tried a manhattan at a restaurant one time and the waiter asked if I wanted it on the rocks. My dad never had a whiskey sour or manhattan on the rocks so I told the waiter no ice. When he returned with the manhattan and I took a sip, I almost breathed fire. It was that strong of a drink.

My dad also would make peppers and eggs, or liver and onions. Peppers and eggs sounded pretty good, but liver and onions? That sounded disgusting. The smell of it was even worse. It stunk-up the whole home. My dad would also make scrambled eggs and home fries. The eggs were all runny and the home fries were never fully cooked. He would ask me if I wanted some and I would take a look and reply, no thanks! Now, the home fries were all symmetrically correct--perfect cubes. My dad would take such time to make sure that they were all similar in size. He was a perfectionist.

His favorite household tool was not a tool. You see, whenever my dad needed to fix something, he used duct tape. Duct tape was used on everything in our house. I bet he wanted to put duct tape across my mom's mouth. If a drawer wasn't on correctly, duct tape. If a piece of the kitchen counter was coming apart, duct tape. And duck tape wasn't just solely used in the house. Nope, my dad used duct tape in our cars.

My dad could fix anything, build anything, and jerry-rig anything. My brother has my dad's skills. Me on the other hand, I could barely tie my shoelaces. I was so envious of my brother. He was so much like my dad. Anything my dad could do, my brother could do the same if not better. Every boy wants to be like his father. I wasn't any different. I so much wanted to be like him, but I really was not like him at all. Well, I had that Italian temper. At the age of 15, when I started to work for my father at the private golf course where he was the greens superintendent, it really showed me a different side of him. He was the boss at work, whereas my mom was the boss at home. He was all business. He had two old Italian men working for him. They spoke broken English, but for the most part they spoke Italian. My father never spoke Italian at home. One day at lunchtime, my father and his two old Italian friends were eating lunch in the garage while I was sitting outside. I heard the three of them speak in Italian and it made me smile. I had no idea what they were talking about. Well, they probably were talking about me. They were probably saying what an idiot I was. That boy can't even tie his shoelaces. Ha ha ha. Then they said one word that I understood, or at least it sounded similar to a word that I had heard before: The F word. The F word in English, is slightly similar to the F word in Italian. I was so happy. I finally knew an Italian word--and the best Italian word you could know.

My father was not a very patient man. The golf course had manual golf carts. They were three-speed with the clutch on the steering wheel, just like an old truck. My father took me out one day to show me how to operate a manual golf cart. That lasted about five minutes. I kept stalling-out. I just could not get the rhythm of pushing in the clutch and putting it into gear and then letting out the clutch while giving gas at the same time. From that point on, I would sit on a golf cart in the garage at the end of a working day and push in the clutch and let it out slowly while the cart was turned off. When my dad would come into the garage, I would get off the golf cart and walk to his truck for the ride home. If I made a mistake during the day, it followed me back home. It stayed with me at dinner time while I ate dinner with my entire family.

One day, my dad told us that he was leaving for the rest of the day. He was going to another golf course to talk to another greens superintendent. I took this opportunity to apply all the lessons that I had taught myself. So I took out the Cushman golf cart and drove it all around the golf course. Up and down fairways, up and down the main driveway, and around the clubhouse. I was having so much fun. I had a big smile across my face and my hair was blowing in the wind. As I drove down the main driveway back to the garage however, there was my dad's truck in the parking lot. Oh shit! I was in deep trouble. I pulled the golf cart into the garage and turned-off the engine. I went into the break room and grabbed my lunch and sat down to eat it. After lunch, my dad would go into that room and tell all his workers what he wanted them to do in the afternoon. He waited to tell me what to do last. I was sitting there all nervous, waiting for him to go off on me. He didn't though. He never said a word to me about the golf cart. Well, he said it in a roundabout way. Saying to me through gritted teeth, you know how to drive the golf cart, right? I told him that I did and he told me that he wanted me to take it out on the course and pick-up any broken branches from the prior night's rain storm. I got onto the golf cart, turned it on, put it into reverse, and then put it into first gear and left the parking lot. As I drove around the golf course picking up branches, I stopped near one of the greens and turned it off. Now, have you ever had the feeling that you are being watched? That's the feeling that I got at that moment. And guess what? I was being watched. By my father! As I turned around and looked over my shoulder, he was literally hiding behind a tree and watching me. Can you believe that? He was watching to see if I could drive the golf cart.

As I got older, my father had me cut the greens and then eventually the fairways. Like I said before, I was not like my brother. My brother started working for my father probably around the age of 15 and by the end of the summer he was cutting greens, fairways, and the rough. Me, on the other hand, it took me three years to cut the fairways. Don't forget that my dad had me starting out painting rocks. Working on a private golf course is a hell of a lot more stressful than working on a public course. On a public course, you have your typical weekend hackers. They probably shoot in the 100s, or sometimes 110s. On a private course, you have members that are paying a steep yearly fee to golf on a pristine golf course. They also shoot in the 100s or 110s, but they look better doing it. They are dressed to the nines. However, thankfully these golfers were not dressed by my mom. If they were, they would have looked just like Rodney Dangerfield in Caddyshack.

When I worked my way up to cutting fairways, it was always a chore for me. Whereas it was like nothing for my brother, it was really difficult for me. It had nothing to do with my vision. I wish I could blame it on that but I can't. I just did not have the touch. If it was a dry day, I had no issues cutting the fairways. If I had to cut it the morning after a rainstorm, it was difficult. This golf course was very hilly and there were a lot of holes where the fairways would go up and down, or slanted to the left or the right. If the fairways were wet and if I was going down or up a hill, the wheels on the tractor would spin. Whenever the wheels were spinning, they would leave a horrible mess on the beautiful fairway. I know that my dad noticed my struggles but he continued to let me cut the fairways. I really don't know why. This was *his* ass on the line, I was just some 18 year old acne-faced punk. I felt so horrible and hated myself for doing that. My brother had no issues with it, but I did. If I was my father and my son did that, I would have taken him off the tractor right away. My dad didn't. He still had faith in me. Maybe he realized that I was a hard worker and wanted to do a good job. I sometimes feel that if I was not his son, he would have fired me. Now mind you, it's not like I messed up the fairways every day. It was once in a while, but it was enough to make me feel horrible and probably enough for my father to let me go.

One time, my friend's father asked my dad if he could give his son a job for the summer at the golf course. My father obliged and my friend and I went out to rake the sandtraps. My friend was doing a shitty job and I tried to tell him what to do but he didn't listen to me. Then I heard the calvary. Here was my dad on the golf cart with his baseball cap placed just above his eyes. I start thinking to myself, "oh shit, dude, you are done. He's going to rip you a new ass hole" Then I started to think to myself, no way is my dad going to yell at my friend because he knows his father. Nope! My dad got off that golf cart just like Clint Eastwood got off a horse, and slowly walked over to my friend. He began by taking the rake from my friend's hand and showing him how to rake a sandtrap properly. I couldn't help but smile. I felt like telling the kid, "dude, I warned you". At least my friend did not have to get strapped like I did when I fucked up. Needless to say, my friend didn't last the week.

There was one time when I was cutting the fairway and my dad told me not to get too close to the green because he would cut that part of the fairway with another mower. So I listened because I didn't want to get strapped (just kidding) and after I got done cutting the fairway, I drove the tractor back to the garage. As I'm driving back to the garage, the general manager of the golf course drove up and started yelling at me. He was telling me that I didn't get close to the green and to go back and finish the job. I didn't take too kindly to this asshole yelling at me, since I was doing what my dad told me to do. I would listen only to my dad, and if he had an issue he should talk to him. Well, here comes the cavalry again. My dad was driving the golf cart with the baseball cap just above his eyes and the general manager in the passenger seat. I'm thinking to myself, shit, I've done it again. I should have kept my big mouth shut. My dad is going to get so pissed at me right now. Quite the opposite happened. I turned off the tractor and he pulled alongside it. He told me to apologize to the general manager. So I did what every good son would do at that moment. I said I'm not going to apologize. You should have seen my dad's face at that time; it just dropped. He was looking at me with those steely blue eyes and they were pleading with me. They were saying, Dennis, please say you're sorry to this man. Seems like the tables have turned, Clint Eastwood. I let my dad squirm for a little bit. I told him that I was only doing what he told me to do. He then told me once again to apologize and I reluctantly said I was sorry. Score one for Dennis.

When I turned 20 years old, I had been working for five summers at THE private golf course. It was becoming too stressful for me to work with my father. Any mistakes that I made, like I said before, would follow me back home. When I told him, he asked me if I wanted to work at another golf course. I should have told him no right then, but I told him yes. I was afraid to let him down. He called a friend of his from another course and set up an appointment for an interview. The day of the interview, I went into his friend's office and told him that I really wasn't interested in working at a golf course anymore. I left his office feeling like shit. The ride home was only 10 minutes but it felt like 30 minutes. I dreaded telling my dad that I turned down the job. So I did what most weak people would do at that moment, I said nothing. I then left the house and went for a long drive. I didn't know what I wanted to do with my life, but I did know that I didn't want to work on a golf course anymore. I really wish that I could have, but unlike my brother, I just did not have the chops for it. I hated that so much. If I could have one wish in this world, it would be to have the skills like my dad.

When I got home, my dad's truck was in the driveway. I had the same feeling as I did when I came down the driveway in that Cushman golf cart at the private club and saw his truck in the parking lot. My heart sank into my stomach. When I pulled into the driveway and turned-off my car, I sat in the driver's seat for a couple of minutes. I did not want to face my father. I was ashamed and embarrassed. When I opened the back door, my father was standing in the kitchen and he was really pissed-off. He turned around, looked at me, and screamed, "why did you turn down the job?" I told him that I didn't want to work at the golf course anymore. He yelled at me again, saying, "Then why the hell did you have me set-up an interview? You made me look bad." And I did make him look bad. He had every right to be pissed-off at me. Although at the time, I was pissed-off at him too. Stupid, right? The man set-up an appointment to get me a job, I turned it down, and now I'm mad at him. What an immature punk I was.

In hindsight though, it was the best thing for my dad and me. Now we didn't have to work together every day and then have to sit at the dinner table and dwell over the mistakes that I made. He didn't have to have me work for him anymore, make mistakes, and then not fire me.

After that, my relationship with my dad got much better and more relaxed. My friend would come over to the house and my dad would be so excited to see him. It's still a joke with my friend and me that whenever my dad would see me, rather than asking how *I* was doing, he would ask my friend how *he* was doing. I joked with my friend that he was the son that my father never had. We had a good laugh over it.

Just as the case with my mother, when Patty and I had Kevin, I understood the hardships that my father had gone through while raising six children. When I visited with Patty and Kevin, my dad would have a big smile on his face. What a contrast from that pissed-off look on his face when I came home from turning-down that job. He would always give Patty a kiss on the lips and a big hug, and he would give me a firm handshake. He would then fake like he was grabbing his belt like he did when I was bad. Just kidding. He never did that. Shit, I acted like I was going to take my belt off and strap him across the ass. That didn't happen but it would be funny if it did.

I believe Easter was my dad's favorite holiday. We had a pretty decent-sized backyard and my dad had a two- tiered garden on the top right side of the lawn. That was his palace. He grew every vegetable imaginable in that garden. He made the Jersey tomatoes look like imposters compared to his tomatoes. They were huge and so juicy.

Getting back to Easter, my dad took pleasure in hiding the Easter eggs. He always had his favorite places. Put an egg in the grill. Put an egg in the downspout. Put an egg in the birdbath in our garden. Put an egg in the gutter. Put an egg in the exhaust pipe of a car and my all-time favorite-- he hid an Easter egg in the ground. Yeah, he dug out a little piece of grass, lifted it up and put an egg under it and then stepped on the grass. As we were all looking for the eggs, he would say such and such was getting warmer, such and such was getting hotter. It always ended with us ripping up the grass to find that hidden egg in the ground. The egg only had a dollar in it but we acted like a $100 was in it, and as adults we would throw our nieces to the ground to find that egg. Who cared if they got hurt? One of the sweetest videos that I ever took, was my mom and dad helping Kevin find an Easter egg in the grill. He had to be no more than two years old.

My dad loved to play the accordion. We all sat around and listened to him play--most of the time out of tune. He loved to throw napkins at an unsuspecting child. He loved to smoke a cigar. He loved to play bocce ball. He loved golf. When he retired from the private golf course at the age of 65, he kept on working by cutting neighbors' yards. He enjoyed the outdoors so much. He probably just wanted to get away from my mom. My mom probably was glad that he was out of the house too.

My favorite dad story of all time was when he was sitting in his truck eating lunch one day and the next-door neighbor came over to complain that my dad had cut too much into his lawn. The neighbor was bitching to my dad that he had cut into his lawn because my dad's lawn looked better than his. The neighbor was an absolute insane, crazy asshole. Now this is where the awesome part of the story gets better and tells you how much of a badass my dad really was. He had to have been at least 85 years old and the neighbor probably was in his 50s. That didn't matter with my dad. As the neighbor is screaming at my dad through the passenger window, my dad is still looking straight ahead out his windshield and slowly eating his sandwich. As the neighbor gets done yelling at my dad, my dad slowly looks over at the neighbor and tells him to get the fuck off my lawn. How beautiful was that? I really wished I was there to hear that. I would have given my dad a kiss on the lips.

Around the time that I had stopped driving, it was brought up to my father that he should stop driving. He didn't stop driving though. He was a very prideful man. He had driven through the neighborhood and hit a couple of mailboxes, so my sisters, brother, and mother told him that he should stop. He was told by his doctor that he should only drive on back roads and not on the highway. Now my dad loved sausage, egg and cheese McMuffins from McDonald's. The problem was that McDonald's was on the other side of West Chester Pike. I'm sure my dad was thinking in his head, I shouldn't be driving on the other side of West Chester Pike but McDonald's is there and damn do I love those McMuffins. They were my dad's kryptonite. So my dad did what he always did, he disobeyed everybody else and went and got his sausage, egg and cheese McMuffin. The problem was though, that morning Patty and I came over to visit him. He knew that we were coming and he said he made us breakfast sandwiches and he was keeping them warm in the oven. They looked just like McDonald's McMuffins. Well, Patty and I found the evidence. I had to throw something away in the trashcan and when I opened the lid, there were the McMuffin wrappers. Here my dad had lied to us by telling us that he had made sausage, egg and cheese sandwiches. Dumb ass. When I told him that he should not be driving across West Chester Pike, he got all pissed-off at me. He put his hand into his back pocket and took out his wallet to show me his driver's license. He told me, "I can drive, I still have my driver's license". When I told him that I still have my driver's license but I'm not driving, once again he got all pissed-off at me. He had been caught.

My dad continued to cut the neighbors' yards into his mid-80s. Didn't matter what the temperature was or how hot or humid. He was always out there in that white V-neck undershirt with the sleeves cut off. In the winter, he would be outside cutting firewood. He never stopped. He was like the Terminator. Unfortunately, time catches up to everyone. It was no different with my dad. Superman was not invincible, and neither was my father. He started to have health issues and spent some time in a nursing home close to our house. That's when my father started to slow down. If not for the health issues, my dad would still be working late into his 90s. It was sad to see such an active man become so immobilized by health issues.

When he moved to the nursing home, I noticed that the sparkle in his blue eyes was gone. I once asked him how he was doing and he replied that he was sad. I asked him what he was sad about and he replied, "everything". That tore my heart apart.

Emily was playing lacrosse for her college team, and my sisters and brother took my father to see one of her games. It was sad to see my sister have to take my father out of the front seat of her car and place him in his wheelchair. The day was cold and he was wrapped in a blanket from head to toe. It was even wrapped around his head. I need to add some levity here because my father looked like Mother Theresa. He enjoyed watching Emily play so much. He loved it when she knocked a girl down. That put a big smile on his face. In his day, he once played football with a broken hand. Superman didn't tell his mother though. Even Superman is afraid of his mother. After the game, Emily, my two sisters and brother stood around my father and took a picture. It's such a beautiful photo. I don't know why I am not in it. I really wish that I had been.

My uncle joined my parents in the same nursing home. There was an area where all the patients would sit and watch TV. Whenever we came to see my dad, he would be sitting in his wheelchair next to my uncle. One time I went to greet him and I got real close and gave him a kiss on the lips, like I usually did when I saw him. This time though, I kissed my uncle by mistake. Stupid vision. My dad got a kick out of that.

Towards the end, my dad developed Alzheimer's. He didn't know who we were most of the time. One time I had a tag on my shirt that stated I was a visitor. When my dad was asked who I was, he said Victorino. I got a chuckle out of that. One time when I was visiting, I went into my uncle's room to say goodbye and it was a particularly bad-vision day for me. My vision was white and I was doing my best to hide my displeasure. My uncle knew I was having a bad day though, and when I said goodbye to him, he grabbed my hand and said to me: "Don't you quit, don't you ever quit!" That shook me a little. Here I thought I was doing my best to hide my sadness but it was very apparent to my uncle.

As it was with my mother, we all knew that the end was near for my father. Every time the phone rang, I would jump to answer it thinking that it was one of my sisters or brother telling me that something happened to my dad. The phone call finally came at 3 AM on September 28, 2012. My sister called and Patty answered the phone. My sister told Patty to get to the nursing home as soon as we could. We got dressed and jumped into the car and drove as fast as possible. That morning my vision was completely white and I was in agony. I had my sunglasses on and sat in the backseat as usual with a blanket over my head. As we pulled up to the nursing home, my sisters and their husbands were entering the building. We walked in together and as we approached my father's room, we heard that horrible sound that most dying people make. It was the same sound that we heard nine months earlier in my mother's room which was right down the hall from my dad's.

As peaceful as my mother had passed, my dad's passing was horrible. When my mother passed, all her children and most of her grandchildren were there. When my father was passing, only his children were there. His grandchildren wanted to be there but we told them not to come. It was that bad. They would have been too upset to see this.

Around 7:30 in the morning, I needed to get out of the room and sit in a dark place. We found a room, with the help of a nurse, and Patty and I went in and sat down. My eyes were on fire. Even though I was in a dark room, it was like a headlight was shining in my eyes. Then most of my siblings joined me in that room. I think they realized the magnitude of how horrible I was feeling.

When my father passed, we were all so upset. This once proud and strong man was no longer with us. Nine months earlier, we were there when my mother passed and here we were again, losing our father. It's always horrible to lose a mother and father, but to lose them in such a short timespan was very difficult. We were lucky that my mother lived until she was 86 and my father lived until he was 92. After he passed we all went back to my sister's house where my nieces showed up with their spouses. I didn't want to go back to my sister's house because my vision was so white and I wasn't in the mood. I sat with my back facing the window in her kitchen with my hoodie over my head, because the light was giving me a headache.

On the day of the funeral, Patty, the kids and I went to the funeral home early. I wanted to be there before all my family arrived. I wanted to have some time to be alone with him. Thank God on that day my vision was just dark, no whiteness whatsoever. When we went into the funeral home, my sister and brother-in-law were there. Bryan was wearing his glasses and my brother-in-law did not recognize him. When they came over to say hi, my brother-in-law put his hand out and said, "Hi, my name is Joe". Bryan said to him, "Joe, it's Bryan". We had a good laugh at that. Joe did not recognize Bryan because he was wearing glasses and Joe had never seen him wear glasses before.

I told my sister that I wanted to see dad alone and she understood. Patty walked me up to my dad's casket and there he was in a suit. The funny thing is, my sisters and brother had him wearing white sneakers. It was hysterical. When I lifted up my dark sunglasses to see my father, the light in the room hurt my eyes so much. I couldn't even see him. It made me so upset that I started to cry slightly. Patty helped me kneel down in front of the casket and I lost it. That was the first time that my children had ever seen me cry and it was really bad. It wasn't just tears-down-my-cheeks crying, I was bawling my eyes out. I couldn't help it. It had been a long 15 months, with losing my mother, losing my job, almost losing my vision at that point, and then finally, losing my father. It was rough.

Once again I stood in the receiving line, this time not seeing anyone. Shaking hands with people that I did not know until they told me who they were. My brother gave the eulogy and he did an awesome job. I was not a pallbearer at this time because I just couldn't do it anymore. On the way to the cemetery the funeral procession passed by the country club where my father had worked. At the gravesite, my sister hired someone to play taps and to give a 21-gun salute. The Marines folded the American flag that was draped over the casket and they gave it to my brother. He was so sweet and gave it to me to have and hold.

The day was sunny and peaceful and warm. It was amazing though because I could actually see just a little bit. I could see my father's caskct and the American flag. Afterwards, we went to the same restaurant that we went to for my mother's luncheon. This time I had the courage to stand up and say something. I said a few jokes and that was about it. When everyone left, we went in the back room and sat around the bar. I took my glasses off and I could see one of my aunt's eyes. Sadly though, that would be one of the last times that what I would ever see anything or anyone.

Chapter 12 - Hanging On By a Thread

The day after Thanksgiving of 2012, my uncle passed away. He had given me a kick in the ass at the nursing home that day, and I will never forget it as long as I live. He was buried with his wife and son right next to the gravesite of my mom and dad. Going to the gravesite the day of his burial, was sad in many ways. He was such a great man and it was sad to see him go, but he lived to the age of 96. Standing near his tombstone, I couldn't help but remember how the past year had gone. We had been to the same cemetery three times. I had not seen my cousins in over 10 years. I had not gone to their parents' funerals because I was such a mess. When I was working, Patty would have had to drive from her work to pick me up and I didn't want to inconvenience her, so I would tell my sisters to give my deepest sympathies.

After my father passed, I had such tremendous guilt. I remember calling my sisters and telling them how I felt and they told me not to feel guilty. It's hard to not feel guilty when you feel like you could have done more but didn't.

Patty figured she would give a call to another neurological ophthalmologist for a second opinion. This doctor worked at the University of Pennsylvania. On October 17, 2012, Patty and I walked into his office not knowing what to expect. You always hope for the best, but at that point I wasn't hoping for anything. When he came in to see me, he took a look at my chart and he kept saying over and over again that "this is horrible". He felt so bad for me. When he took a look at my eye, he told me that I was hanging on by a thread. That scared the living shit out of me. I knew that my vision was bad. I knew that I was slowly going blind, but to hear a doctor say it like he did and the way that he did, almost dropped me to my knees.

One day Patty and I were watching a medical program and a doctor from Boston was featured. He was explaining an issue that he had with one of his patients about a year ago. His patient had uveitis and was slowly losing her vision just like I was at that point. This doctor was one of the best uveitis doctors in the world. I had never heard of him before and the program caught our attention. He was describing how his patient was losing her vision, but it was not related to anything in her eye. It was something else in her body. After she came into visit him, he told her what he thought the issue was and told her to see a specialist. When her condition was diagnosed, she was treated and her vision slowly came back. I remembered the doctor's name, and when the neurological ophthalmologist told me that I was hanging on by a thread, I asked the doctor if I should go to see this doctor in Boston. He told me that I should go as soon as possible.

Patty and I went home and called the doctor in Boston to see if I could get an appointment. When we called the office, the nurse told Patty that they had an appointment for the following day at 7 AM. We were shocked. It was almost like a divine intervention had occurred. What are the chances that they would have an appointment for us the following day? I honestly thought that it was my mother intervening from above.

Our car at the time was old and had a lot of miles on it, so I suggested to Patty that we rent a car. All of this was going down so fast. Patty called a rental car place and secured a small compact car for the drive to Boston. Kevin drove us to the rental car place and wished us luck. We threw our duffel bag in the backseat, got into the car, and sped away. The trip to Boston would take us five hours and we wanted to get there as soon as possible. When we left Pennsylvania, it was almost 4:30 PM.

As we drove on the New Jersey Turnpike, we crossed the George Washington Bridge and then eventually drove into Connecticut. We stopped and went through McDonald's to grab a couple of burgers and continued on our journey. I could barely see at that point. My vision was so dark. The shade not only was coming from the top left, it was now coming up further into the bottom of my eye. I could barely see as much as a penny-sized circle. Patty and I were both apprehensive and excited at the same time. This was my final chance to correct my vision. It was this doctor, or nobody else. I was mad at myself for not thinking about going to this doctor earlier. It was now or never for both of us.

As we neared Boston, we were slowed to a crawl because there was an accident on I-95. The traffic near Boston is bad most of the time, but we did not think it would be bad that late at night. At the rate that we were going, we would arrive at our hotel at midnight. We were both so mentally and physically exhausted at that point. We had gotten up early in the morning to go to Philadelphia to see the neurological ophthalmologist, and now here we were stuck in traffic an hour outside Boston. We were both getting antsy and cranky.

We eventually pulled into our hotel just before midnight. We grabbed our duffel bag and ran into the lobby with me holding onto Patty's arm for dear life. We eventually got into our hotel room 10 minutes after midnight. It took us close to seven hours to get to Boston. We quickly got into our pajamas and rolled into bed. I remember lying in bed wide awake, hoping and praying that this long journey would be fruitful.

The 6 AM alarm came so quickly. It felt like we had only slept for an hour. I probably only did sleep for an hour because I was tossing and turning all night. I was thinking about every possibility that could happen. Maybe he would tell me there was something that could be done for me. Maybe he would tell me that there was nothing that could be done for me. How would I handle that situation?

His office was right next to the hotel, so Patty and I walked out the main entrance of the hotel and took about a two-minute walk to get to the office. It was a really big room with a lot of chairs. There were already a lot of people waiting to see him. From what I gather, he had people from all over the world going to see him. He was the real deal. Now at this point I had been going to see eye doctors for over 11 years. I had been in so many waiting rooms it seemed like I had spent a third of my life waiting to see a doctor--whether it be an ophthalmologist, retinal specialist, glaucoma doctor, neurological ophthalmologist or a world-renowned uvetis doctor. However, this wait was unique. This was the big leagues in my mind. This was the end of the road for Patty and me.

It seems like we waited for an hour, when in reality we only waited about 15 to 20 minutes. When my name was called, I grabbed onto Patty's arm and she walked me into the doctor's office. His office looked like any other doctor's office that I have been to over the years. But this felt much more different than the other visits. Sitting in the chair, my legs kept shaking up and down, I was visibly nervous and Patty knew it. She was nervous as well. Just then the doctor came into the room.

The man that I had seen on television, walked into the room and handed a note to one of his assistants. I was confused. He didn't come into the room and say hi to me like most other doctors had done. Then the nurse read the letter. She said the following: "the doctor has laryngitis and his doctor has told him that he cannot speak for the next week". I'm thinking to myself, what the fuck? We drove over seven hours to Boston to see this uveitis specialist and he can't speak to me? Are you kidding me? Is somebody playing a joke on us? Nope! There was no joke. He really did have laryngitis. What is the possibility of that happening? Anyway, he looked over my chart and then took a quick look at my eye. He didn't take too long to look at my vision so I kind of figured that he had nothing to say. Maybe he would just pat me on the shoulder and let his assistant tell me what he thought.

But that's not what he did. After he looked at my chart, he wheeled his chair around to me and said in a raspy voice, "I'm sorry but I know that you drove a long way to see me and you wanted to hear me tell you what I thought. Even though it's against my doctor's orders, I figured I owed it to you to tell you what I think. Your vision will never get any better. It's as good as it's going to get". I'm sure that this doctor had seen so many patients over the years that I can't even fathom the number, and I'm sure that he had to tell a lot of them the same news that he told me. He could have gone through the motions though. He could have acted like Dr. Idiot and not given a shit about me. That's not what he did. He was total class. He had such empathy for my situation. Before he left the room, he told me that he didn't want me to live the rest of my life lying on a couch. "A lot of people have gone through what you are going through, and they live their lives to the fullest. I want you to do same."

I wore my Philadelphia Phillies 2008 World Series champion hoodie to the appointment. After the doctor gave me his sermon, he asked me why I drove for seven hours wearing that silly sweatshirt. He made a joke and it made me laugh. He was really good like that. After telling me something so dreadful, he followed it with a joke. What a really good doctor. I just wish that I had found him sooner but I hadn't. Just like that, he was gone. The appointment lasted no more than 10 minutes.

Patty and I took the long ride back home. We sat in silence for most of the ride. We stopped in Connecticut to grab something to eat and I really didn't want to talk. It was devastating news. We thought we had a chance with this doctor, but we didn't. The end of the road was upon us and we both know it. What was left for me was to go blind. I was so scared and I didn't know if I could ever do what the doctor asked me to do. Don't lie on the couch the rest of your life? That was what I was thinking at that moment. I am going to lie on the couch for the rest of my life and never get off it. I can't do this, even though my mother said I was strong enough to do it, I just wasn't going to do it or maybe I just didn't want to do it. I was going to take the easy way out.

When I got home, my sister called me up to see how the doctor's visit went. I couldn't talk. When I started to open up my mouth, I knew that I was going to cry. I didn't want to cry in front of my sister. I wanted to act strong but I just couldn't handle it. I started to cry and then she thankfully told me to call her back. I didn't though. I stayed on that phone and I cried. She felt so bad for me and wished that she could do something to make it better but there really wasn't anything that she could do.

I hung-up the phone and went into my bedroom, lied down, and just cried. It was one of the saddest days of my life. I had so many sad days in the previous year, but this one was ranking right up there with the worst. I went downstairs and gave Patty a big hug and told her that I was so scared because I was never going to see her again. She tried to assure me that I was going to be OK, but I wasn't having it. After I gave her a hug, I went upstairs in our master bathroom and sat on the floor, grabbed my knees, and balled my eyes out. Sitting on the cold tile in the dark, I prayed to my mother to help me have strength. I was at the end of my rope.

I was starting to think that the number eight was an unlucky number for me. Everything over the last year had an eight for the day. For instance, my mother passed on 8 December, my father passed on 28 September, and now the horrible news from the doctor in Boston on 18 October.

Just as it was in 2011, Christmas 2012 with a very solemn occasion. We were over at my sister's house once again and I was sitting on the couch next to Patty while everybody was opening their gifts. My great niece, who was three years old at the time, was bringing over gifts to each person and when it was time for her to bring a gift over to me, she looked up at me and asked so sweet and innocently, "why can't you see?" That broke my heart. What can I say to her? How could I describe what I had just gone through over the past 11 years? I kept my composure and told her, "it's a long story sweetheart; one day when you get older I will explain". Heck, at that point it was difficult to explain it to an adult. It was that complicated. My situation was so rare that my doctors didn't have enough experience to correct the problem. Every time I saw a doctor, no matter who it was, he would say that my issue was complicated or that he had never seen anything like this before. That's comforting to know.

Chapter 13 - Hitting Rock Bottom

There was a movie released in 1967 called, "Wait Until Dark". It starred Audrey Hepburn, Richard Crenna, and Alan Arkin. I remember watching it on television, probably in the early 1970s. The Academy Awards nominated Audrey Hepburn for best actress. If you remember it, she played someone who had just lost her vision and was living in an apartment with her husband. Men knocked on her door, came into her apartment, and acted like they were friendly strangers, when in reality they were con men. When her character finally realized that they were crooks, she removed all the lights in her apartment. She was able to get a knife and stab the crooks. However she had forgotten about the light in her refrigerator. The crooks used a dish towel to block the door from closing. She was so determined to get away that she pushed the refrigerator away from the wall, unplugged it, and hid behind it until help arrived. Her thought process was to even the playing field and have the crooks see exactly what she was seeing. She knew her way around the apartment because she was blind, but the crooks were at a disadvantage. In early 2013, I felt that same fear. Not so much with strangers coming into the house, but what if they did. Would I be able to defend myself? Would I be able to defend my family? The fear in Audrey Hepburn's character was very relatable to me at that time. Her husband was away on a business trip and was not there to protect her. She was all alone in that apartment to fend for herself, and the crooks knew it.

Like I said before, in 2013, Patty was working, Kevin was commuting to college, and Emily and Bryan were away at college. So I was home alone every day. One morning when I woke up, I got out of bed and started to have this tremendous panic attack. It was something that I had never experienced before and it really disturbed me. My vision was almost nonexistent and I felt this tremendous fear of claustrophobia. I tried to calm myself down, but nothing worked. I was walking around the house in a complete panic--grabbing my hair and pulling it, while screaming. I almost felt like I wanted to open a window and jump from the second story of our house to make the pain go away. It was that bad. I called Patty at work. I'm sure every time I called her at work she was expecting the worst. I told her about my panic attack. She tried to calm me over the phone but it didn't work. I just kept screaming and crying that I wanted it all to stop. She told me to go into our pantry and take out "tension" tea bags, heat some water in the microwave, and put the teabag in the mug to let it steep for a while. When it was done, I should drink the tea and it would calm me down. When I opened up the pantry though, I realized that I could not distinguish which box was the tension tea, so I went into my father-in-law's apartment and asked him for some help. I did not tell him what the real reason was for the tension tea. At this time, my mother-in-law was in an assisted-living home near our house, and he was living by himself. He would sit at home most of the day and either listen to music, watch television, or read a book. He came in and helped me get the teabag and then he asked me if I needed anything else. I told him that I was fine, which I was not, and he went back into his apartment. I heated the water in a mug in the microwave and then let the tea steep. While all of this was going on, I was freaking out. It felt like my heart was beating 200 beats a minute. The tea really did not help. I spent the rest of the day just walking around the house nonstop. When Patty got home from work, I had drunk about three or four cups of tension tea and it finally kicked in. After we ate dinner, we sat down to watch TV. Around 6:30, I passed out and slept for the rest of the night. I thought when I woke up the next day that that panic feeling would go away, but it had not. I believe that the reason for my panic attack was that all options had been explored to make my vision get better and I knew that there was nothing left. Eventually I would just go blind. I really do believe that put me off the deep end. It was a very scary feeling to not have any control over myself; to think that the only way to stop my panic attack would be to jump out a window.

I spent almost all day at the house and never went outside, or to any events, or to anybody's home. I couldn't handle it. I couldn't handle going blind and I just could not handle going out and losing control, or the fear of losing control, like I did at home that one morning. Patty had been invited to a jewelry demonstration at my niece's house and she wanted to go. I was conflicted because I didn't want her to drive by herself, which was an hour away, but I did not want to leave the house at all. My sister was having a party before my niece's jewelry demonstration, So Patty and I stopped by. The thought process was that I would stay at my sister's house while Patty went to the jewelry demonstration, and then afterwards she would come back, pick me up, and drive me home. It all sounded so normal, something that I would not have hesitated to do in the past. I was not normal at that time and I was petrified. Even though I would be around my family, I just did not feel comfortable. I did not want to get a panic attack in front of them. They really did not know how bad my mental state was at that time and I wanted to keep it that way. I thought I could handle all the shit by myself.

Patty made me a big travel cup of tension tea and we went to my sister's house. She stayed there for a little bit and then left. Now, at that time, Patty was my comfort. Patty was my normal. Patty was my strength. Basically,

Patty was my everything. I told my sister, reluctantly, what I was going through and the purpose of the travel mug. She understood and told me that if I needed to, I could sit on a chair in her living room. I sat down at the kitchen table with her and my brother-in-law's family. After a while, I was starting to slowly get uptight. I stayed there for a little while trying to fight the panic but finally I told my sister that I needed to go in the other room. She was so sweet and she guided me into her living room. I asked her to turn all the lights off because that would make me feel more at ease. At that moment, I barely saw that much light, but just the fact of knowing that all the lights were turned-off made me feel more comfortable. I could hear the others talking to one another, laughing, and having a good time. I was just so miserable. I tried to fight it, but the tears started to fall down my cheek. There had been so many happy times at my sister's house, but this was definitely not one of them. This was not good. I was starting to lose it again and I was afraid. Afraid of losing it in front of my sister and brother-in-law's family and freaking them out. My sister came in occasionally and asked me how I was doing and I would lie and tell her that I was good. Thankfully Patty did not stay too long at the demonstration, and came back to drive me home. I cried the whole way home. I didn't know what to do to stop this panic attack. I thought I was going nuts.

At this time, I was bitter. Man, I was so goddamn bitter. Bitter at the world. Bitter at my family. Mostly, bitter at God. I would lie in bed at night and talk to God. "Why are you doing this to me, God? Why me? What the hell did I do to deserve this?" I would also pray to my Mom and Dad and ask them to make this go away. I was hanging on for dear life.

My anger at God got to the point where I called a priest at a local church and asked him if he believed in the theory that "everything happens for a reason"? I asked him, "What reason would there be for me to lose my vision?" He told me that he did not believe in that theory and he gave me words of comfort. I also told him that I did not believe in people who think that if they pray to God, things will get better. He told me that he believes in free will. Free will is leaving it up to people to live their life as they please. It's not God's fault when something happens, it just happens. Basically people are in charge of their life and are responsible for the mistakes they make, or the choices they make. It was my choice not to go to the eye doctor every six months. It was my responsibility to wear glasses and not walk into a chain and have it come back and hit me in the eye. That was all on me, and not God. Once I got over my anger with God, I needed to find a way to get over my anger at everybody in my life.

Whenever my sisters would call to see how I was doing, I was so damn miserable and angry. I yelled and screamed on the phone. Not angry with them or at them, but I needed to vent. They would listen and try to understand the best they could, or give me words of wisdom or assurance. It got to the point where it was every time they called me. I'm sure that it was dreadful for them knowing what to expect when they would call. They had no idea the hell I was going through and nothing they said would make it any better. I was that defiant. I was almost blind, and I was done with all of it.

To add some levity to this chapter, one day I was lying on the couch watching television or should I say *listening* to television. The remote control was on the floor and as I reached for it to change the channel, my pinky tip hit the rug and I heard a crack in that finger. I immediately felt severe pain. I thought that the pain would eventually go away but it didn't. When Patty got home, I told her what I had done and she brushed it aside. She told me that my finger was probably broken and there was nothing the doctor could do for it--just tape it to my ring finger and deal with it. So that's what I did. I dealt with it. I went outside and I cut some branches off my neighbor's pine tree with my two fingers taped together. I dug out a shrub that my mother-in-law had planted in her garden with my pinky and index finger taped to each other. Afterwards, my finger was on fire. We made an appointment with an orthopedic specialist and he told me that I had torn the tendon at the tip. I just laughed out loud. I couldn't believe I tore the tip of my pinky ligament by reaching down and grabbing for the remote control. I wish I had a cooler story to tell. Like I got in a bar-room brawl with Brad Pitt.

The doctor referred me to a hand specialist who made a small plaster cast to put over the tip of my finger. The cast had two Velcro straps and a buckle that would keep the cast tight on my finger. I also went for physical therapy to gain mobility. It was an absolute joke though. Having this little plaster cast on, going out and having people ask me what I had done--only for me to tell them that I had hurt my pinky while reaching for the remote. Dumb ass.

In April, I started to talk to Kevin about having a surprise 50th birthday party for Patty. She did all our finances and there was no way that I could take money out of our bank account for a down payment at a restaurant without her knowing any of this. I asked Kevin if he could put the down payment on his credit card. He told me that he would and then I asked him if there was any way that Mom would find out, and he said no. We found a nice restaurant in downtown Newtown, and put a down payment on his credit card. I had Kevin grab Patty's cell phone when she was not looking and give me the phone numbers for her friends from high school and her friends from work. I texted these friends and gave them the date and time for the surprise birthday party. I then reached out to my family and did the same. The total of people invited to her surprise party was 50. Everything was going smoothly as planned. Then we encountered a glitch in our operation. Patty is a sleuth, like Nancy Drew in one of her mystery novels. One day Kevin's credit card bill came in the mail and guess who got the mail that day and opened the bill? Yup, Nancy Drew. Why did Nancy Drew do that? Who knows. Nancy, I mean Patty, was in the kitchen when she opened Kevin's bill; I was in the family room. She then proceeded to ask me why did Kevin spend X amount of dollars at X restaurant in Newtown. I played dumb, which is easy for me to do by the way. I told her that I had no idea and she should talk to him when he got home. Meanwhile, I was so pissed-off at Kevin. He told me there was no way that Patty would find out, and now she did. Kevin came home shortly after that and Patty grilled him. Man, she was grilling him like Erin Brockovich. I wasn't in the kitchen to see that, but I bet sweat was starting to form on Kevin's forehead and slowly going down the bridge of his nose. I have to give it to him though. He held steadfast to his story. His story was that they had made a mistake on the bill. Patty would not relent though. She told him to go upstairs and call the restaurant and let them know they made a mistake. He went upstairs and closed the bedroom door. I'm sure he was in that room trying to come up with a plan.

Kevin then opened his bedroom door and ran down the stairs and into the kitchen. As he walked by me, I just shook my head like my Dad always did. I almost wanted to go into the kitchen and tell Patty that it's for your surprise 50th birthday party! I wanted to tell her that we tried to surprise you, but you were too damn smart to be surprised. I didn't though. I wanted to see how this would play out. It was like I was in a soap opera and the soap opera was called: "As the Shit Hits the Fan". Kevin told Patty that he called the restaurant and they had made a mistake. They had added an extra zero to his credit card. Patty then asked him what he was doing at that place on a Monday. He told her that he had gone to the restaurant to grab a drink with his friend. All was good with our plan. Kevin had saved the day. Patty on the other hand, was concerned that Kevin was an alcoholic, which he is not.

The day of Patty's surprise party, she went out for the day with her friend. Her family, my family and her friends gathered at the restaurant awaiting her arrival. I was there, with my manly pinky cast trying to explain to everyone what had happened. The restaurant had supplied a buffet and everyone was getting drinks at the bar. It was a really good time. Just then, Emily received a text from Patty's friend telling her that they were five minutes away. Everybody gathered into the far left of the room and waited for Patty to enter. Now like I said before, Patty was such a smarty-pants and thought that she could never be surprised. Guess what? I surprised the hell out of her. When she entered the room and everyone yelled surprise, her jaw dropped. I got her! It was awesome. Everyone came up to her and gave her a big hug and kiss. She deserved it. She had been going through hell with me for such a long time and now she was having issues with her mother. She is one strong woman. I stood up to give a speech and my sister was videotaping me but I had no idea. She told me afterwards that she had, but I could only see black and a light shade of white. When people came up to me, I'd had no idea who they were. I acted like I knew them but I didn't. It was only about 10 or 15 seconds into talking to them that I realized who they were by their voice. Both my nieces have the exact same voice and I had no idea who they were. It was only when I hugged them that I realized who they were because one niece has long hair and the other has short hair. I even got lucky that night. OK, let's not get carried away.

Emily grew up playing soccer, and like I had said before, I coached her for a little bit. When she got to high school, she tried-out for the high school team but did not make it. She was devastated. Luckily though, her friend was trying-out for the lacrosse team and they were looking for athletes. This was the second year of the high school girls' lacrosse team and they really didn't have many players. Emily was reluctant at first, saying that she had never played lacrosse before. I told her that if she could catch a softball, then she could catch a lacrosse ball in the air. So Emily went to the high school, tried-out, and made the team. OK, they were looking for anybody at that point. She didn't exactly try-out for the team. They were looking for girls who could walk, breathe, and chew gum at the same time and Emily fit that bill. Hell, every girl fit that bill.

As my vision slowly dwindled, it got harder and harder for me to watch and enjoy Emily's lacrosse games at high school. She got a limited scholarship to play at a Pennsylvania college and when she played there, my vision got so bad that I had to ask Patty where she was on the field. Every girl on the lacrosse team had her hair in a ponytail and Emily was no different. In her senior year of 2013, my vision was so bad that I had to watch her games through binoculars. During one game, her teammates said out loud that there was some pervert on the other side of the field watching them with binoculars. Emily told them that it was her father, and that he was blind. Well, I was legally blind at that point. I'm sure it was embarrassing for Emily. Her friends felt so bad. She had never told them that I was blind. Emily is a very private person, like Bryan, Kevin, Patty and me. She didn't want to bring any attention to herself. As the game was going on, Patty would announce the game. I used to enjoy watching Emily play lacrosse, so this was devastating.

In May 2013, my niece and her fiancé got married at a local country club. This was the first wedding after my dad's passing and I wanted it to be special for my niece. I was given one of my father's suits after he passed and I thought it would be cool to get the suit altered so I could wear it to the wedding. This way, a piece of my dad would be there. When I got the suit altered though, the crotch was a little tight. Sorry dad. Just keeping it real here. Just kidding. Anyway, the wedding was a lot of fun and my niece appreciated my wearing the suit. I have to say though, my dad danced much better in that suit than I did. The only sight I saw of my niece that day was a white blur. I could not see her face at all. I did my best to have a good time though. She and I danced to AC/DC's *You Shook Me* and that's a memory I will never forget. The best memory however of that wedding, was what transpired afterward. Let's just say that most of the people at the wedding got a little hammered--some more than others. We all decided to go into another room of the clubhouse to take a family photo. As we were walking up the stairs to the second level, one of my nieces (I will not say who but she knows who she is, and everyone else in our family knows who she is) grabbed onto my arm because she was a little unsteady. She wanted me to guide her. Me! Me, who is blind. Seriously? That's what I said to her too. "Are you kidding me? You were holding on to me? You must really be hammered!"

In June 2013, Patty the kids and I went to Ocean City for a vacation. Now Ocean City, New Jersey, is my favorite place in the world to visit. It is not the most glamorous but it is the most comfortable for me. Like I had mentioned before, all my sisters, their families, and Lieutenant Mom would go to Ocean City for a week. I would love to go to the arcades. The problem I had was that no one was my age. I started to go to the shore with them when I was 12 years old. I loved to play crazy climber, gunsmoke and ski ball. I was given an allowance, but I blew through that very quickly. I wanted so bad to play arcades, that I snuck into my sister's and aunt's room and grabbed any loose quarters they had on top of their bureaus. Yeah, true and full disclosure. I did that. So now you know. Can't get mad at me now though. It's past the statue of limitations.

So when I got older, I wanted to vacation in Ocean City with my own family. Patty and I and the kids started going when Bryan was around two years old in 1995--lugging all the beach toys, beach chairs, beach blankets, duffel bags, and coolers to the beach every morning at 9 AM and staying until 5 PM. It was laborious, but I loved it. At night, we would walk to the boardwalk and either do the rides, play arcades, or play miniature golf. Always though, the night had to have soft-serve ice cream—preferably chocolate. Now at that time, Patty and I were trying to vacation on a budget, so we could not afford the really expensive ice cream. Emily could not understand that. Every time that we walked past the expensive soft-serve ice cream, she would cry and say I want ice cream! And each time we would have to tell her that we could not afford that and that she would have to wait. We walked 10 blocks to the inexpensive soft-serve ice cream store and then she was happy. This happened every night for the six nights we were there.

There is a photo of Emily, Bryan, and me on the boardwalk. Patty took the photo from behind us and it's me in the middle of the two of them and I am holding their hands. Bryan was probably three and Emily was probably five years old. It's a really cute picture and one that I will always remember. There is another photo of me on a bike with Bryan in the seat behind me. We are both wearing helmets and Bryan was smiling, but you could tell he was scared shitless. Of course in every shore photo of Bryan, he looked scared shitless--whether it was on the back of the bike with me, on the beach with sand on his hands, or at the top of the Ferris wheel.

Now in 2013 when we would go to the boardwalk in the morning, I could barely see my kids. When we went on the beach, I would sit in a chair and just listen to a book on my Discman. They would be throwing a football around and running in the water. I couldn't do that and I was very sad. They then wanted to play wiffleball and asked me if I wanted to play. So I joined them in their game. I got up to the plate and got in my batter stance, just like I did when I was in my Mom and Dad's backyard. This time however, I couldn't see anything. It was all white. Emily threw the ball and Bryan would tell me when to swing. I got so disheartened that I just stopped. I had Bryan walk me back to my chair and I just sat down and allowed them to continue what they were doing. At night on the boardwalk, instead of me walking between Bryan and Emily and holding their hands, I walked between them and held onto their *arms*. As I walked past the Mac and Manco Pizza Shop, the Waterpark, the King Kong Miniature Golf, Playland, and Wonderland, I couldn't see any of it but I could hear it. I would just visualize what it was like when I was a 12-year-old and walking on the boardwalk looking for an arcade to play gun smoke and crazy climber. My favorite thing to do on the boardwalk, was to go up at night, sit on a bench and look out toward the ocean. Just listening to the waves crash onto the shore, was so peaceful for me. Now, when I sat on the bench and looked out towards the ocean, once again I couldn't see anything, but I could hear. It was the same, but once again it was different. It's funny sometimes how life can be the same and so different at the same time. Here I was in the same place as I was when I was a young kid, as I was as a young parent, and now as I was as an older parent with grown children.

The funniest thing that happened that week did not happen in our house or on the beach. It happened at a restaurant near the bay in Ocean City. Friday night, Patty, the kids and I went out to eat and we sat in the back of the restaurant. Bryan had to guide me to my seat. The restaurant was packed and the tables were really close to one another. After we got done, I grabbed onto Bryan's back and he led me in between the chairs and the tables so I would not bump anybody. As we got to the front door, I grabbed onto his arm and walked out the door. I put my left arm out to the left to grab onto a railing that was not there. As I put my arm out to the left, Bryan started to yelled "no, no, no," with each "no" getting louder and louder. What I did not realize was that there was a woman off to my left who was coming into the restaurant as we were leaving. If Bryan had not grabbed my arm and pulled it away, I would have grabbed her boobies. Bryan apologized and she understood and just laughed. As we walked away, Patty said to me, "Den, her boobies were big too".

When we got home from vacation, my bitterness and anger were still there inside me, right at the surface ready to appear at any time at any place. It was very stressful at home for everybody. Finally, it all came to the surface, and it was not good. We had a family discussion at the dinner table one night. This was always where we spoke about our day and what was going on in our lives. It didn't matter when--at breakfast, dinner, lunch, or the occasional late-night snack. We all sat down and listened to each other's day and tried to comfort one another. This talk was different than the others. Whereas before, everyone would speak and each one of us would listen and give our thoughts, this time it was them talking to me. They had had it with me, and I had had it with them. They all took turns voicing their displeasure with me and my attitude, and I got real defensive and yelled back at them. It wasn't good. Kevin started crying and told me some issues that he had had with me for a long time. I got mad and yelled back. Finally, I just lost it. For the second time in my life, I cried in front of my kids. It wasn't good. I told them that I had hit rock bottom and that I needed to get help. For the longest time, Patty, the kids and my sisters were telling me the same thing. You need to get help, but I just didn't listen. It wasn't until I decided that I needed help, that I went for help. However. I waited much too long to do so. I just was so scared. Patty would tell me that other people were going through the same thing that I was going through, but I just didn't care about their problems. I just cared about mine. Nobody understood what I was going through. In my mind, I was the only one that was going through this.

In October 2013, another niece was getting married on the beach in Ocean City. My sister got our whole family a rental to stay in for the weekend. It was just like the old days when we all stayed in one house together with my Mom bossing everybody around. This time however, my Mom would only be there in spirit. The weekend before the wedding, I went to my eighth grade's 35th class reunion. I had not spoken to most of my classmates in over 35 years since they went to a different high school than I did. Patty took me to the restaurant in my hometown, and I was nervous. At that time, I really had not gone out anywhere. I felt horrible about myself and who I had become. When I went into the restaurant, one of my good friends from grade school came over immediately and introduced himself to me. He did not mention anything about my disability, so this put my mind at ease. We talked about the old times and then he took it upon himself to introduce me to everyone at the event. It was a really sweet thing for him to do. He had no idea that I had lost my vision and he made an effort to make me feel comfortable. However, as the night went on and I had spoken to most of my classmates, Patty and I were left standing on the back deck of the restaurant next to one another. Everyone had branched off to their friends. I told Patty that I was ready to go. I felt uncomfortable. So I said goodbye to everyone and one of my friends told me that he was really proud of me and that I was very strong to come out in public the way I did. That made me feel great. That lifted my spirits. What a kind thing to say. He didn't have to say anything, but he did. It made a difference.

Back to my niece's wedding in Ocean City (I know that I jump back-and-forth a lot in this book but that's just how my mind works). Anyway, I was so excited for her and her husband. It was such a beautiful day, at least that's what we hoped it would be. The forecast called for thunderstorms and it was not looking promising for them to have their beach wedding. As the day progressed, my sister made an announcement that they decided to have the wedding inside the house. The bride and groom were bummed out, but they made the best of it and it was a beautiful ceremony. Bryan and Emily did a great job singing songs that the couple liked.

After the ceremony however, that's when I finally lost it. I had hit rock bottom. Unlike the previous time when I was all alone during my panic attack, this time I lost it in front of my family, my niece's husband's family, and my niece's father's family. I lost it in the place that I love to go to during the summer. The place that had given me such joy over the years, was now the place for my most sorrow of sorrows. I started to cry uncontrollably. Patty tried to comfort me but it just didn't work. My sisters noticed me crying and came over and tried to comfort me as well. Here was my sister, at the wedding of her daughter, and I was crying. I felt so selfish and foolish and stupid. My niece who had just gotten married, came over and tried to comfort me as well. Nothing worked. I was just so sad. What put me over the edge, was that I just could not see what was going on. I wanted to see how happy the bride was on her wedding day. She had been through so much in the previous 14 years, and this was the day that she deserved.

I told Patty that I wanted to go back to the house instead of going to the reception, but she told me there was no way that was going to happen. I pleaded with her but she didn't listen. My sister told me that she wanted me to introduce the wedding party at the reception hall. I told her that I was in no mood to do that. She kept on insisting, so I relented and said yes.

On the way to the reception, I felt horrible. I felt so stupid and I felt that I had ruined the wedding. It had come upon me at such an inopportune time. My sadness just overwhelmed me. As hard as it was for me to keep my composure, I just couldn't do it. The worst part about it was that I had done

it in front of a lot of people. A lot of people who did not know me, and a
lot of people who were family and just did not know what to do to make it
better. I think that's when they realized the magnitude of my problem. I
had done such a good job of masking it over the years but now it was out
in public for all to see its ugliness. I had no more excuses. I needed to get
help and right away.

I did as my sister asked and introduced the wedding party just like that old-
time public announcer for the Philadelphia 76ers, Dave Zinkoff,
accentuating the vowels and consonants in the names of each usher and
bridesmaid. Finally, I introduced my niece and her husband. That made me
feel good. The rest of the evening was great. I got down on my knees and
danced with my cousin's daughter. For one evening, I was better.

Chapter 14 - I'm Learning To Walk Again

I don't remember the exact date that I lost my vision. All I know is that it was gradual. One day I woke up and I was blind. I knew it was going to eventually happen, but when it did it still caught me by surprise. It was strange.

During the 1992 winter Olympics in Albertville, France, Nancy Kerrigan's mother had to get real close to the television to watch her daughter skate. She didn't sit in the stands, she stood real close to a television in the arena. It was sad to see, although the joy on her face after she saw her daughter perform in the Olympics was very touching. I had experienced those same feelings while watching Emily play lacrosse, or Bryan perform in a play or musical in high school--not to the extent that I had to sit on the stage, but I needed the aid of binoculars to watch Emily play and I needed Patty's help to tell me were Bryan was during a performance. When Kevin graduated from college, I needed Patty to let me know when he walked by us to go on stage to get his diploma. I was glad that I was able to be at the big moments in my children's lives, but also was sad that I was not able to see them.

I was told by my doctor that my blindness was caused by advanced glaucoma. By taking oral prednisone for so many years, it caused the pressure in my eye to go up and down. This eventually damaged my optic nerve. I had mentioned the possibility of having retina replacement surgery, but was told that the risks outweighed the rewards. Not to mention, it was an extremely bloody surgery. What had happened to my left eye was what you would call a perfect storm: uveitis, followed by high pressure, followed by the weakening of the optic nerve, and then finally blindness. This was an extremely rare disease that had caused me to lose vision in both eyes.

When I was younger, whenever I saw a blind person on television or in person, I always felt bad for them. I felt like they were different from me. It was only when I became blind, that I realized that they weren't different from me, they were the same as me, except they couldn't see. You always feel like you are better than someone else who has a disability, but you really are not. I wasn't any different than anyone else growing up. Now I was the blind person. I should have prepared myself for this, knowing that eventually I would become blind, but I didn't. I was running scared from being blind and it caught up to me.

The conversation that I had with the doctor in Boston about not living my life lying on a couch was ringing in my head. Patty telling me that I could live a full life while being blind was ringing in my head. My Mom telling me that I was strong and I would be fine, was ringing in my head. What was I going to do? Once I lost my vision, it was almost like I was a baby once again. I had been reborn as a different person--a blind person. It sounds even weird saying it out loud right now. I was that person I had seen on television, or in person at the mall, or anywhere out in public. When I saw someone who was blind, I would look at them because they stood-out from everyone else. They had sunglasses on and a walking stick, or sometimes a guide dog. I always wondered what they were thinking, and now I knew what they were thinking. Or at least I thought I knew. At that point in my life, I was not thinking like a courageous person. Not thinking like that courageous person who was walking through the mall by himself with a walking stick or a guide dog. That person was courageous. Me? Not so courageous at that point. Actually, I was a very terrified young man. I should say a very terrified young child because that's how I felt inside. I felt like that child who was afraid to let his mother's hand leave his when he went to kindergarten for the first day. That child who was afraid to let go of his mother's hand when he got on the school bus for the first day of first grade. That was me. I was born again. Not in the religious sense, but in the growing-up sense. A child who was experiencing everything for the first time. How would I handle that? Would I be able to cope with it? These were the thoughts that were running through my head.

I eventually came to terms with the fact that I could not stay inside my home for the rest of my life. I needed to do something to make it better. I knew what I had to do for the longest time, but I kept putting it off. Just like when you were in school and kept putting-off a book report or an essay. You would wait until the last day, or the morning of, to finally complete your assignment. Well, the clock was running out for me. It was the day the report or assignment was due. It was now or never with me. I had become almost unrecognizable to what I once was as a man. I used to be so fun to be around, although Patty may disagree with that statement, and loved to have a good time. I loved to have a good laugh with friends and family. I loved to be sarcastic and tease people. That wasn't me anymore. I didn't know if I would ever be that person again.

The first thing that I wanted to do was to feel better, to stop feeling so damn sad all the time. As soon as I woke up in the morning, that blindness would be right there with me until I finally went to sleep at night. It prevented me from having any semblance of enjoyment in my life. I wanted to get that back so badly. With the help of Patty, we found a psychiatrist and he prescribed anxiety and depression medication. That was a big step for me to take because I thought that if you had to rely on medication for happiness, you were considered weak. The medication took about two weeks to take effect and when it did, I felt such a great relief. This however was a minor step to getting back to feeling better. I needed to talk to someone about my problems. I know this is a very sexist thing to say but that's how most men are brought up to feel. They are brought-up to feel like they were strong and didn't need anybody to help them out with their problems. Macho-man talk, bullshit talk actually. This was the reason for me not getting help for such a long time. It was the reason why I was in this situation in the first place. I had put-off going to my ophthalmologist to get my retina checked-out and how did that turn out for me? Now, I was holding-off on talking to someone.

I researched every psychologist in the area and eventually found someone that I liked based on the profile. I am a shy person by nature. It takes me a while to get used to someone, but when I do I can become myself. Most people who know me would disagree with me being shy. It's the truth though. It's my way of protecting myself from being hurt.

I felt right at home during the first meeting that I had with my psychologist. It was not awkward at all. She was a very nice person and made it comfortable for me to open-up and talk, without being judged. She let me do most of the talking. Now I know that's what psychologists are supposed to do, but I had gone to a psychologist in the past, where he did most of the talking--relating his issues in life to what was going on in my life. Maybe that was just how he operated, but it didn't help me at all. In hindsight, I really believe that I was resistant to any help. This was not related to my vision problems. This was related to work issues. I truly believe that if you're not open to change then you will never change. I was not open to change at that time. I basically just wanted to bitch and moan about what was going on in my life. It really is true what they say, right place and right time. That was the situation with my therapist.

The therapist asked me a few questions to start and then it was off to the races for me. I talked the whole session and when she said that the session was over, I was surprised. It felt like I was only talking for 10 minutes, but in essence it was 45 minutes. It felt really good. This was the first time that I had talked about my issues with someone who was not related to me. I could tell her how I was feeling and not get shit in return. It felt like a weight had been lifted from my shoulders. Actually, a huge weight had been lifted from my shoulders, because I knew that I could talk to her and she would listen. Not that Patty, my kids, or my sisters weren't listening, but this felt much different. There was no "but" following a reply by my therapist.

With each subsequent visit, more shit that had been lying inside of me for such a long time, came out. I had so much anger inside me. So much sadness inside me. So much resentment inside me. My therapist had taken a can opener, and took the lid off all those emotions and they popped out of me like a snake in a novelty-store can. I told my therapist about how some people had told me that they could do a better job dealing with being blind. I think that was the most difficult thing for me to hear anyone say. How can anybody say that to someone who is blind or going blind? How do they know that unless they are blind? At night, I would hear that phrase over and over again in my head. This would cause me to tear-up, and then eventually my tears would find their way down my cheek to my chin, and down my neck. How do you reply to a statement like that? I had basically been told by my manager at work that I was faking it, and now someone was telling me that they could do better than I was doing?

I don't know if this is an Italian thing or not, but when I met Patty, I felt like it was my place to protect her. When my kids were born, it was my place to protect them. That's why I punched that bastard in the back in Washington DC. That's why I got so mad at that soccer dad who gave Patty shit. That's why I would get pissed-off at Kevin or Bryan's friends when they were treating them badly. That's why I would talk to my daughter's coaches whenever I felt like they were upsetting her. As my kids got older, I still protected them. Even though they were teenagers or young adults, I still took it upon myself to protect them. After talking this over with my therapist though, I realized that I couldn't do that anymore. It wasn't healthy and it really didn't help matters. Your children have to learn on their own. They have to be accountable for their own mistakes. In the song, *Long Time Coming*, by Bruce Springsteen, there is a line that applies to me during those sessions with my therapist. It goes as follows: *I pray that your mistakes will be your own, your sins will be your own.*

After months of going to therapy, I eventually felt at ease and at peace with myself. I allowed myself to take a step back and allow my wife and children to handle their problems without my intervention. I would always be there for them if they needed me. I slowly learned that the best way to help them out, would be to listen, not to talk. For an Italian, not talking is like taking off an arm.

The next step to my path back to a healthy life, was to go to a place where everyone knows my name. Just kidding. I needed to go to a place where everyone was in the same boat as I was. There was a blindness center right around the corner from where I lived. I had been there before, but not inside the building. Attached to the building was a thrift store. Now just the mention of thrift stores brings me back to when my mother dressed me in that red and white checkered picnic-table-looking shirt. It sends chills down my spine. I would have looked better wearing a potato sack to school than that ugly damn shirt. I can't stand shopping. I don't even go into the stores anymore with Patty. I sit in the car and listen to my phone. So there was no way in hell that I was going into a thrift store because this would bring flashbacks. So she would go into the store and I would sit in the car and wait for her to come out. I would wait and wait and wait and wait and wait. It felt like she was in there forever. It felt like she picked up every piece of jewelry, clothing, or appliance in that shop. It got so bad for me that I actually almost got out of the car to go into the store and ask her what the hell was taking her so long. Eventually though, she would knock on the trunk and I would pop it open for her to pile in all the bags that she had with her.

One day, my father-in-law drove me to the center to meet with a social worker. At the time, I was taking medication and was seeing a therapist, but this was the trifecta. I needed to hear what other people were going through. I had a really nice meeting and the social worker couldn't have been any nicer. She told me about the programs that they had and there was no pressure on me to go but that it would be a good thing for my recovery. I left the center feeling upbeat and willing to give it a shot. My father-in-law then asked if he could go in the thrift shop and I told him that I was going to smack him across the face. Just kidding.

My sister was learning transcendental meditation and she mentioned to me that it would be a good idea if I did the same. I always have a lot of shit going on in my head and I didn't feel that meditation would be something that I could do. She told me that transcendental meditation is not about stopping you're thinking but letting your thoughts pass through your head and then relaxing. Once again, I figured that it would be something that could help me. My mind now was open to trying anything to get me back to happiness. I have to admit that the first time that I went to see the Director, I was a little uneasy. She told me about the program and what it entailed. I would meet at the center for three straight days to go over the program with other people. At that point, I would be on my own. The female Director worked with the women and the male Director worked with the men. I was told the background of transcendental meditation and what famous people were using this form of relaxation. People like Jerry Seinfeld, Howard Stern, and Paul McCartney. I liked all of them so I figured if it was good for them then it would be good for me.

I was told to bring a white handkerchief and a piece of fruit as an offering for the ceremony. I thought that was a little kooky, and it was much kookier when I brought those items to the center. I was given a mantra to repeat over and over again while I was meditating. I am not at liberty to share this mantra with anybody. Patty doesn't even know the mantra. OK, I will now reveal my mantra. It's called, *none of your fucking business*. No, it's not that. I was told that I should meditate for 20 minutes in the morning and then 20 minutes in the evening. It should be done while sitting up and it didn't necessarily have to be done in a quiet place. You could actually meditate while a passenger in a car. I never tried that but I would imagine that it would be extremely difficult to meditate while listening to heavy-metal. The purpose of transcendental meditation was to get pure awareness. I know it sounds like I'm getting deep here, but pure awareness is where you were actually so deep into meditation that you don't hear your mantra. You are at total peace. I accomplished that one time. It was only for a few seconds but it was like I was back at Emerald Lake in the Rocky Mountains. While I was meditating one time, my jaw started to move up and down, so much so that my teeth were chattering. It was like I was freezing but I wasn't cold. The purpose of meditation is to take an area of your body that is stressed out and to relax it. Remember when I talked about how my dad always gritted his teeth when he was angry? Well, I guess at that time my jaw was tense most of the time and this meditation was relaxing it.

I felt like a completely different person. I was never a relaxed person. I am the guy sitting at the table with his leg moving up and down 50 miles an hour. Now, I was at total peace. I was so happy once again. Nothing bothered me.

Unfortunately, there are always bumps in the road. Nothing is as rosy as it seems. You always see people post something on social media saying how happy they are, but in reality they are just hiding their true feelings. I was experiencing a down moment in my life and I did something that was really stupid. At these down moments, you feel like life will never get any better. Even though tomorrow is another day and you get another chance to make what's wrong, right, you feel that you'll never be OK. I would take three pills for my anxiety during the day. One in the morning, one in the afternoon, and one before I went to bed. I took one pill a day for my depression, and I took that in the afternoon. However, for reasons that escape me now, I was having a particularly bad day. One of those days where I just didn't wanna get out of bed. One of those days where I just did not think that I would ever feel any better. At that time, I had a pocket between my mattress and box spring where I kept my medications. I opened up the anxiety medication, and instead of taking one pill, I took three. Sounds stupid, right? Yeah, it really was a stupid thing for me to do. Like Brian Johnson in the *Breakfast Club* bringing a flare gun to high school in order to commit suicide. I was giving up. I was so ashamed of myself as well. After I did it, I was so scared. I can't believe I had done that. I lay there in bed and just cried once again. I haven't cried like that in a long time. Here I was thinking that I was getting better, when I was just lying to myself. The sad thing is that I knew that I could do this. I knew that I wanted to get better. I knew that I was getting better, but I had a bad day. It could have been worse, but nothing happened. Thank God nothing happened. If it had, then I would not be here telling you my story. It was a very selfish thing to do.

So I had that setback, and I was never going to do that again. I always search for solace in lyrics to songs. That's where I get my happiness, my strength, and my peace. I don't read poetry, but lyrics to a song are poetry. There are a handful of bands that I will buy a CD without even listening to it. Obviously one is Bruce Springsteen. The others are Tom Petty, Bryan Adams, Counting Crows, and Foo Fighters. One of my favorite Foo Fighters' songs, and there are many, is called *Walk*. Every time I hear this song, I tear-up. It brings me back to my bedroom that sad day and it makes me realize how much life has to offer. Life has a lot to offer you if you're willing to open up your hands and take it. Like I said before, I felt like a child when I lost my vision. I felt like I would never be the same person I was before. The lyrics in the song spoke to how I was feeling at that time and afterwards. They are as follows: *I am learning to walk again. I believe I've waited long enough, where do I begin? I am learning to talk again. Can't you see I've waited long enough. Where do I begin?* Then at the end of the song, it says the following, *I'm on my knees I'm praying for a sign. Forever, whenever, I never want to die, I never want to die.* That's how I felt. I was ready to move-on. I did not want to die. I was not going to give-up the fight. I was not going to quit.

I mention Bruce Springsteen a lot in my book. My brother gave me my first Bruce Springsteen record on my 16th birthday. It was, *Born to Run.* Once I heard that album, I went out and bought all the albums that he had. *Greetings from Asbury Park, The Wild, The Innocent, and the E St., Shuffle, Darkness on the Edge of Town,* and *The River*. His lyrics have such depth to them. They could apply to anybody. Those lyrics apply to me during rough and good times. There was a particular song that he wrote called *Wrecking Ball*. At the end of the song he says: *hard times come and hard times go; hard times come and hard times go.* Just like the Foo Fighters' song, *Walk*, those lyrics get to me all the time. I remember seeing him in concert playing that song and I was singing along with him and tears were rolling down my cheeks. Those lyrics were speaking to me, telling me that hard times come in your life and they will go just as fast as they came into your life. Then as soon as those hard times go away, new hard times come in. That's life in a nutshell. You either deal with your hard times or you let your hard times deal you a bad hand. It's all in how you approach your life. Even today, when I hear those two songs, they bring tears to my eyes because I think back to that weak, scared, child lying in bed trying to end all of his pain. Isn't that what music is supposed to do? Isn't music supposed to be enlightening? Music is extremely powerful and it is extremely powerful in my life.

I'm going to make reference to the Bruce Springsteen song *Long Time Coming* again. In that song, he writes the following lyric: *I'm going to get birth naked, bury my old soul, and dance on its grave*. That's what I was doing. I was reborn, once again. Any time that I went out in public for the first time, whether it be to go out to dinner or to an event, it was as if I was a newborn trying something for the first time. Although every experience was wrought with fear. You know that when you walk into a room with sunglasses on, people either think that you are a pompous asshole or you are blind. In my case though, my sunglasses were so big (honestly Jackie Onassis' sunglasses) that people knew that I had either gone to the eye doctor and had drops put into my eye to make my pupils dilate, or that I was blind. Even though I could not tell, I felt like every eye in the restaurant was on me. I felt bad for Patty and the kids because they could see people's reactions. I know there were a few times that Patty and the kids got mad at people for staring at me. But I was that person when I was younger, staring at someone who was blind. I guess it is a natural reaction for someone to look at a person who is different.

Chapter 15 - I'm Not the Only One

The first day that I went to the Association for the Blind and Visually Impaired (referred to as the Center), it was one year and one day from when my mother passed. While waiting in my family room for the driver to arrive, I sat pensively. I was so nervous, just like a little kid on his first day of school. Would people like me? How would I get along with the other kids? I was scheduled to be picked up at 8:30 AM, but I was ready around 7 AM. I had my lunchbox next to me on the couch and my shoes all tied and ready to go. I was wondering what lay ahead.

I had pushed aside going to a support group for such a long time. Rather than trying to listen to what other people had going on in their lives, I chose to sit at home and bitch. This was a huge step for me to admit that I could not do this on my own, and that I could not put the burden of my issues on the shoulders of Patty and my kids. It was not fair to them. They were not professional social workers working with someone who was legally or completely blind.

When the driver arrived, I nervously grabbed my lunch box and walked through the foyer to our front door. As I opened the door, the driver said hello and in a very friendly manner which put my mind at ease. We started talking about sports and we got along very well. At the first stop, a woman got into the van and asked me what my name was. She put my mind at ease. At the second stop, a blind woman got into the van and asked me if I was training to be a new driver. I got a chuckle out of that and told her that

I was a new client. I said that if I was training to be a new driver, they would be in some serious trouble.

When the van finally made it to the Center, the driver got out and helped everyone into their seats. I sat next to an older gentleman who was very friendly. He asked me what my name was and what my eye condition was. I tried to explain, but he had never heard of it before and I just gave up. At that point, other vans from other locations arrived and the room got rowdier. Everyone in the room was friendly, and I just sat there and listened. I felt like a new student who had arrived in the middle of the school year. A few people who were sitting close to me, asked my name and introduced themselves to me. I felt like I was at home even though I had never met these people before.

When everybody had settled down and the clock read 10:30, the social worker that I had met before with my father-in-law, entered the room. She brought with her such a kind and relaxed attitude. Everyone reciprocated her emotions back to her. There was a friendly banter between her and the clients. My approach to this first meeting would be to sit back and listen to everyone talk about their lives and to blend-in with the walls. I didn't want to be noticed and I thought that was what was going to happen. When the meeting started, my social worker told everyone that there was a new client and to go around the room and tell what their eye condition was and their name. As I listened, no one had an eye condition like mine. I heard of clients who had gone legally blind due to retinitis pigmentosa, macular degeneration, Stargardt's disease, or a stroke in their optic nerve. As the clients talked about their issue and told their name, it eventually came around to me. I told them my name and my eye condition. I was not surprised that most people had never heard of it before.

As I got done speaking, I breathed a sigh of relief. Thank God I got that out of the way and could now just sit back, relax, and listen to what the social worker wanted to discuss with the group. However, that did not happen. She started to ask me questions. I got a little flustered because like I said before, I am a shy person. These were people that I had just met and now I had to open up to them right off the bat. I was a little uneasy, to say the least. They didn't know who I was, and I didn't know who they were. How the hell are they going to help me when they don't know what I am going through? I came across a little bit (OK very) defensive. When I spoke about my issues and how I was feeling, I was extremely apoplectic. I probably was a bit of a prick. I told the group that I felt like nobody knew what I was going through and no matter how hard I tried to tell them, they didn't understand or didn't want to understand. Here I thought I was only going to speak for a couple of seconds, but when I got done speaking it was about five minutes.

Once I got done venting, a handful of people started to tell me their experiences and that this was an open environment where you could share your feelings. They told me that they had experienced the same emotions that I was going through. It was normal to feel the way I was feeling and I should not be ashamed of myself. The meeting lasted about an hour, and when it was over the social worker thanked everyone for coming and went back into her office. Everyone started to talk amongst themselves while they ate lunch. I sat there quietly listening to everyone laugh. I felt uncomfortable starting a conversation with anyone. A couple of women came over to me and started to make conversation. They were so nice, as was everybody at the Center that day. Another woman came over to me and asked me when my birthday was because she made homemade birthday cards for each client for their birthday. I thought that was so sweet of her. The only downside to the whole meeting, was that there were only a few men there to talk about my favorite topic, sports. They were on the other side of the table from me except for the older gentleman next to me. However, he left the room at lunch time.

The driver came into the meeting room and helped everyone back into their respective vans. The drive home was enjoyable, with everyone getting along. When the driver pulled into my driveway, he helped me out of the van and up to my front door. As I unlocked the door, I shook his hand and told him I appreciated all his help. He responded with no problem and that he would see me next month. As I shut and locked the front door, I took off my jacket and put it on the banister and then brought my lunchbox into the kitchen. I let out a sigh of relief. I had done it. I had gone to a group therapy session and made it out alive. I walked back into the family room and lay down on the couch and quickly fell asleep. I was so mentally and emotionally exhausted.

When Patty came in the kitchen from the garage, she asked me how my day went. I was like a little kid after his first day of school. I ran into the kitchen, jumping up and down and saying "Billy was nice and Tommy was nice and Timmy was nice". I didn't do that. However I was excited. I felt so comfortable that I wanted to go back right away. However, these group sessions were only once a month. They had other programs that the clients went to, but I was not ready for that yet. Then Patty and I went upstairs and made whoopie. No, that did not happen. Let's not get carried away here.

Notice a trend here?

I kept thinking about that group meeting the whole week. It really opened my eyes to the fact that I was not the only one that was going through this. There were people who were in worse shape than I was. People who had their eye condition since birth. People who had never driven a car before. People who were fine one day and then the next day they had lost most of their sight. Even though all of that happened to them, they still seemed upbeat and optimistic. They were living their lives to the fullest extent. Yes, they were angry about their lost vision, but they had learned how to deal with it. Every emotion that I was feeling, they had felt before. They were in my shoes at one time. They were the new client at the Center. They were the angry one who didn't think there was anyone else that was going through what they were going through. They understood me.

By the time the next month rolled around, I had lost all my anxiety and was looking forward to going back. The same people and the same driver were in the van. They made me feel so welcome and at home, but I still was not completely myself with them. I still had a lot of anger inside me, and they were open to hearing my pain. As was the case with the first meeting, my social worker came-up with a topic and went around the room so each client had a chance to voice their opinion. Once again, when it came to me, I gave a short reply but she asked me a follow-up question. I thought to myself, Jesus, I feel like I am on the witness stand with my mother when I didn't go to church. I replied with a bit of an attitude--even though I was on medication, even though I was meditating, even though I was going to a therapist. Whatever she was talking about, struck a nerve with me. Talking to a therapist, allows you to speak freely. Talking in a group session with your peers, everyone is going through what you're going through or have gone through in their life. So here I thought I was the only one, when in actuality I was one of them.

It was funny to bring up stories about how people act when a blind person is around. Someone brought up about how people will talk louder to a blind person even though they are not deaf. Another person brought up how when you are with your spouse at a doctor's appointment, the nurse or doctor will talk to your spouse not to you, even though it is your appointment. Then there is the person who will come and sit down next to you and sit there for a while, then get up and walk away without telling you. You then find yourself talking to an empty chair. Sometimes you are standing and someone will come up next to you and talk. At some point though, they will walk away. This once again makes you look like an idiot because you were standing there talking to an imaginary person.

Every scenario that was brought up, I had been there and done that. It was a light-hearted atmosphere and I really enjoyed the banter. It was never that serious of a meeting. For the most part, everyone had a lot of laughs. In the end, I think that's what everybody needed. We needed to laugh because if we're not laughing then the only thing that's left to do is cry about our situations. Not to say that there weren't moments when people got choked up, because there were many of them. That's where the other clients came in to reassure the person that everything would be OK. It was one big family where everyone could speak their mind, and their voice would be respected. There were also times where people got on each other's nerves. That type of thing happens in almost every family. That's when the social worker's calm demeanor brought the topic back on track.

I have to say that even though I was on medication, even though I was meditating, even though I was talking to a therapist, the most important person in my life, besides my wife and children, was my social worker. She was a godsend for me at that point in my life. Now I'm not going to say that she was a saint because she had a devilish streak in her, but she was the best. She was not a rah-rah type of person--rather a person that you felt comfortable telling your every emotion. With each subsequent meeting, I felt more and more at ease to raise my hand and add to the topic of discussion. I think she appreciated that because as someone who is facilitating a meeting, you want to feel like people are inspired by your voice. I don't think that any other person at that time in my life would have lit a fire under my ass like she did. It was the right place at the right time once again for me, I truly believe that if I had lived in another county and had gone to another Center, I don't think I would have been able to do most of the things that I did after meeting her. I owe it all to her. Now I hope that when she reads this, she doesn't get too huge of a head. I mean it's praise from me, and who the hell am I?

The list of appreciation does not start and end with my social worker. There are so many people at the Center who helped me out immensely. People who gave me their cell phone numbers and allowed me to call or text them whenever I was having a tough time. People who saved a seat at the Center for me to sit next to them. People who would give me a big hug when I was having a hard time. I also appreciated those who gave me shit for continually acting angry and feeling sorry for myself. That was the best kick in the ass that I ever got. "Stop feeling sorry for yourself. No one in here is going to feel sorry for you because everybody else is going through the same damn thing." Isn't that the type of conversation that families have at the dinner table? Wasn't that the type of conversation that I was having at my dinner table? You bet it was. They were my family, as was the case with my wife and kids, I would defend them at any cost to anyone. They were my blood now. They were part of me. How could I let them down? I wasn't going to let them down. I was going to make them proud of me. I damn sure was proud of them.

I took a little piece of each of them and applied it to my life. I put myself in their shoes instead of having them fit into mine. I sat there and learned empathy and compassion. I listened to how they would deal with the situation. How they handled losing their vision. How they handled someone who was rude to them. I put all that together like a big jigsaw puzzle. After about six months, I started acting like myself. As was the case with most people who got to know me, they could not believe that I was the same person that walked into the Center as a bitter man. I was teasing people. I was being my normal sarcastic self. I was laughing. I was me again. It wasn't like I was not still upset about losing my vision, because I was, but I was learning how to deal with it. That was the whole purpose of the support group. Everyone there knew that they weren't going to get their sight back again. Everyone was there to have some outlet for their sadness.

The first thing that a blind person will tell you they miss the most, is driving a car. I heard that over and over again at the Center. No matter what the topic was, they missed driving a car. They missed the independence. They missed the spontaneity. They missed getting the middle finger from a pissed off driver. I missed going through the Wendy's drive-through at lunch time, and getting a double with cheese and bacon, cheese fries and a Dr Pepper, then driving back and parking my car in the parking lot of my job and listening to the sports-talk station.

It was sad to hear how people were treated by their family. How they were treated like children because they had lost vision. How their family did not have any patience for them. How their family did not show any respect to them and left crap on the floor for them to fall over. What astonished me the most was, that people were living by themselves. I couldn't believe that, considering how much I leaned on Patty and the kids for everything. They were the most courageous people that I have ever met before in my life. Someone was actually babysitting her grandchildren by herself. Try doing that with vision and then do that blindfolded. I dare you to. That's really impressive.

People who lived by themselves, would take an Uber or the para-transit to their doctor's appointments or to meet up with friends for dinner. They would go to the grocery store or take a walk around their apartment complex. There were people who would take a trip to the pool for the afternoon with the aid of their walking cane and nothing else. Well, they had a bathing suit on, but you get the point.

Then after about a year of going to the Low-Vision group, my social worker suggested that I should go to a group called Adjustment to Blindness. Almost all the people in the Low-Vision group were legally blind and my social worker thought that it would be a good idea to go into a group meeting with people who had the same issue as I did. The Low-Vision group had about 20 people each month, whereas the Adjustment to Blindness group was a much smaller group with only six people. With a smaller group, it was a much more intimate environment and everybody got a chance to speak their piece each month. There was one man who was living by himself and would attend church each week. There was another man who was born with a tumor behind one of his eyes and as he got older, he needed a glass eye in his other eye. This did not stop him from cooking dinner each night or fixing lawnmowers or any other engine that needed to be repaired. There was another man who was in a horrific car accident and in a coma for six months. He lost his vision and was living alone. Not to mention that he was a diabetic and had to give himself insulin injections daily. One man lost his vision at 16 but that did not stop him from graduating college and becoming a minister. One man was in a motorcycle accident where he rolled over the hood of a car. Not only did he lose his vision but he also had a foot amputated.

I was their peer, but they were my idols. How amazing their determination was in the face of such severe adversity. They were living alone and relying on only themselves to do what I was relying on Patty and the kids to do for me. I never heard them complain. They only talked about the positive side of life. Each of them imparted their wisdom to me. I found out how they dealt with normal everyday activities. How they used their other senses instead of relying on their vision. With the Low-Vision group, besides one other woman, I was the only blind person in the room. With this new group, we were all dealing with the same problems, but it seemed like their problems were much more difficult than mine. How can I complain? I lost my vision at the age of 49. I was born with a lazy eye, not born with a tumor behind it. I did not lose my vision at 16. I wasn't in a horrific motorcycle or car accident that left me in a coma. My vision loss was gradual. Now losing your vision is no picnic, but at least I had time to prepare. Some of these people had no time to prepare. One minute they could see and the next minute they woke up and they couldn't. How traumatic that must have been for them.

One woman in the group had to deal with the passing of her husband. She relied on him just like I relied on Patty. However, she now was left having to rely on her daughter. One woman I got really close to in the group. She was a sweetheart. One day the Center took us to a bowling alley. They provided us with shirts but we couldn't have stuck out any more because the shirts that they gave us were bright yellow. The color of a highlighter. Everyone who went to the bowling alley, had already been assigned a team. That left me and three blind women on the same team. Now, the other teams either did not have any blind people in their group of four, or had one.

Two of the women in my Adjustment to Blindness group were on my team. Where the other teams had a total of over 250 points amongst the four of them after one game, our team had 70 points with me having 51. Our team had a lot of fun though. We had the most gutter balls.

Sadly, the one woman I had grown very close to, passed away from a sudden illness. She was too young to die. Do you know what they say, only the good die young. I missed her so much as did the rest of the group and the entire Center. This was not an isolated case though. There were many more people whom I had grown to know and admire, that passed away. It was like losing a family member. It was that deep of a loss. The times when we would meet, their absence was felt by everyone in the group, including the social workers.

Story, after story, after story astonished me. How brave these people were. Would I ever be that brave? I didn't know at the time. All I knew was that after more than ten years, I was feeling better and happier than I had ever been. Everything that I accomplished from that moment on, I owed to my social worker and every person I met at that Center. That was the center of my life. They will all be like family to me for the rest of my life. I owe them more than they will ever know. They welcomed me with open arms as a broken, angry man, with warts and imperfections --no questions asked. The chapters that follow, would not be possible without them. Thank you to my brothers and sisters. I love you all.

Chapter 16 - Up All Night

One night after my mother had passed, I could not sleep so I went downstairs to lie on the couch in my living room. It was one of those nights where everything was running through my head and I could not get to sleep. It was around 1:30 AM when I went downstairs, and I probably got to sleep around 3 AM. At least I thought I was sleeping because have you ever had a dream where you are in the same room in which you were actually sleeping? I never have and I truly believe that I was awake when this strange scenario happened. I was lying on the couch in the living room facing the front windows and the end table with a lamp on it. All of a sudden, the lamp turned on and started to levitate horizontally. I have heard that spirits will connect to us through electricity. This may have been one of those occasions where my mom was trying to connect with me because I was having an extremely difficult time. Who knows? Maybe I was dreaming and imagined all of this, or I was wide awake and this actually happened.

I also would feel movement on the bed during the night--almost like someone was sitting on the mattress next to me. This would occur more frequently after my father had passed. I believe that this was my mom and dad's way of letting me know that they were there whenever I needed them. Call me crazy, but I truly believe that this was what was happening. I was having such a difficult time dealing with grief, guilt, and sadness--not to mention anger about being fired from my job.

Gradually, I started to wake up almost every night after sleeping only a few hours. I would lie in bed wide awake and could not get back to sleep, so I would go downstairs and lie in the family room. I didn't want to go back into the living room because it kind of freaked me out thinking of what had happened that one night with the lamp levitating. I would toss and turn on the couch trying to get back to sleep, but nothing worked. Finally it would be morning and Patty would come down to eat breakfast before she went to work. She would get up around 4:30 AM so she could leave for work around 6:00 AM. After I ate breakfast with her, I would go back into the family room and lie on the couch. Eventually, I would fall asleep and sleep most of the day. At night, we would go to sleep and I would only sleep for an hour or two and then be wide awake. After tossing and turning and trying to get back to sleep, I would get out of bed and go downstairs to lie on the family room couch once again. This began to be a nightly occurrence: me waking up and not being able to sleep, then going downstairs and lying wide awake waiting for Patty to come downstairs to eat breakfast before she left for work. After she would leave, I would fall asleep for most of the day. She went to a doctor's appointment one time and brought this up to her doctor and he came up with a great idea: try staying awake all day. Well Dr Obvious, don't you think I am trying to do that? Gosh, I wish everything were that simple. He also said to be more active during the day and to ride an exercise bike. I tried that but I was just so exhausted that no matter what I did, I would just lie down on the couch and fall asleep. Patty and the kids were getting annoyed with me not being able to sleep at night. They would try to help but nothing worked. It would get to the point that I actually dreaded night because I knew what would happen when I lay down on the bed.

Now, when I was younger I sometimes had difficulty going to sleep. I remember my sister having to sit on my bed and bounce up and down on the mattress. I guess this soothed me enough that I would eventually fall asleep. Patty still does that for me to this day. Just kidding.

I tried to take melatonin at night to help me fall asleep, but that did not work. I even went for a sleep- study evaluation at our local hospital, but all I did was lie awake in bed while the guy probably read comic books. In the morning, the guy came in and said I had never witnessed someone not sleeping at night. I tried drinking wine before I went to bed, but that didn't help. Basically everything that I tried to help me fall asleep, did not work.

When I started to date Patty, I would visit her during the week after I got done work. She lived an hour away from me so my friend said that she was geographically undesirable. When I got to her house, I would eat dinner with her family, stay for a little bit and eventually drive back home. I would sometimes wake up in the middle of the night after coming home from her house and have a dream that I was pushing the brakes of my car, but they weren't working. Then I found out that I was seated in my bed with my right foot pushing the footboard of my bed.

When I was around 16 years old, I was lying on my right side in the fetal position with my right arm hanging off the bed. I had a dream that I was being pulled under the bed and I woke up screaming. In my dream I got startled and my left hand grabbed my right arm in order to save me. I let out a scream and then realized it was only me that was doing it. My mother came upstairs to see what was going on and I told her what had happened.

My father was probably still in bed shaking his head and muttering silently to himself, "what a dumb ass".

When Patty and I were first married, we slept in a double bed in our apartment. One night, I had a bad dream and grabbed Patty and started to scream at her, "who are you? who are you?" This startled her and she screamed which made me wake up. When we first had Kevin, we would have him in bed with us before we went to sleep. Patty would wake up and see me sitting in bed with my hand searching the mattress. When she asked me what I was doing, I told her that I was looking for Kevin. Another time she noticed me sitting in bed and rocking an invisible baby. Another time, she woke up to me standing over her with my legs straddling her and my hands were on the wall above our bed. I had a dream that the walls were falling on us and that's why I was doing this crazy shit.

So you can see that whenever my head hit the pillow, no matter if I was 16, just married, a new parent, or dealing with blindness, I always had difficulty sleeping. I guess this runs in our family because my sister would wake up and have night terrors when she was eight years old. My dad would pick her up and bring her into the bathroom and splash water on her face to help her wake up. If you have ever experienced someone having a night terror, it is scary because they are looking at you but also looking straight through you. Their eyes have a distant look. When Emily was around six years old, she started to have night terrors. We tried everything to avoid her having them. We had her go to the bathroom before she went to sleep. We gave her warm milk before she went to bed. Nothing worked though. We would lie in bed and wait for her to wake up. We thought that if we could get her out of bed and awake, this would prevent her from having a night terror. That didn't help either. I would bring her into the bathroom, just like my dad did with my sister, and splash water on her face or have her look at her reflection in the mirror but that didn't work. Eventually she grew out of that phase, but it was not pleasant for us or Emily.

After Emily got over her night terrors, that's when Bryan started to have some issues with falling asleep. His bedroom was next to ours and we would have to leave our bedroom door open and our light on. This way he would be reassured that we were there for him. After an hour or so, I would get up out of bed and turn off our bedroom light. Just as I got back into bed however, I would hear Bryan call out "Mom?" When Patty would answer him with, "what Bryan?", he would reply, "nothing". Then being the kind and patient father that I was at that time, I would tell Bryan to go back to sleep and Bryan would answer with a nervous and scared "OK".

One day at the Center, my social worker brought in two people who were familiar with blind and legally- blind people who have difficulty sleeping at night. There was this condition called non-24. I had seen commercials for this on TV and was interested in it because it seemed like that was something that I had. They described why blind people may have a hard time sleeping at night because their circadian rhythm is off and they can't distinguish between nighttime and daytime. They told us that there was a medication that you could take that would correct this problem. At that time however, taking another pill was out of the question for me. I was already on depression and anxiety medication and was starting to experience the side effects of being on oral prednisone for years. This was just another issue that I would have to deal with on my own. Every other night, my optic nerve would be misfiring causing my vision to be completely white, like someone was shining a flashlight directly into my eyes. This made it almost impossible for me to go to sleep. Try getting to sleep with the lights on in your bedroom. That would be difficult. Now try to sleep with a light as bright as a tractor trailer's headlights in your vision. That's what I was dealing with every other night. The nights when my vision was dark, I still couldn't get to sleep. I tried everything but nothing worked. The nights when my vision was white and I fell asleep for a couple of hours, I would wake up with my dream in my vision due to Charles Bonnet Syndrome. I was beginning to feel like a vampire--up all night and sleeping all day. What made me feel at ease, was that a few people at the Center were experiencing the same difficulty at night. The days when I went into the Center, I would be so tired at the end of the meeting that I almost fell asleep at the tables. When I returned, I threw my lunch bag on the counter, lay on the couch, and fell asleep until Patty got home. The first thing that she would say when she came in the house was "did you sleep today?"

Like most men do each day, I would read the sports page from front to back. I would even bring the sports page to work and read it in my favorite place. If you are a guy, then you know what that place would be. My friend once came to my desk to borrow my sports page. When it came back to me folded- up differently, I knew where he had brought it. I asked just for certification and when he told me where he brought it, I threw it in the trashcan. I was not going to read that tainted sports page.

When the kids were young, I would read them the comic section from the Sunday Inquirer. I would make up different voices while reading and the kids enjoyed it a lot. Patty? Not so much.

When my vision slowly started to dissipate, it became much more difficult for me to read. By this time, all my kids were teenagers and they did not want me to read the comics to them anymore. When I would ask, they would run away from me. When I asked Patty, she did the same. My doctor recommended low-vision reading glasses. Now these puppies aren't your regular reading glasses that you get at the dollar store or pharmacy. Those glasses are for amateurs. The glasses that were prescribed to me at the low- vision center were puppies that could burn a hole in the sidewalk if sunlight went through them. With the aid of these glasses, I was able to read again. I could read the sports page in my favorite place at home or read a book. Before, I would need my kids or Patty to read the sports page to me, not that I minded that they did it but it's so much better to read it yourself in your quiet place. These glasses were so powerful, that Mr. Magoo could use them when driving.

I started to dictate an audio diary using my iPad. I talked about what had happened to me each day. It served two points. One, it gave me something to do and two, it allowed me to vent. This got boring after a while and I thought I could apply my emotions to a much better purpose. So I decided to write lyrics. One of the greatest songwriters of all time, Warren Zevon, once said that his lyrics were half fiction and half nonfiction. This was the model for my lyrics. I tried to describe the emotions that I was going through at that time into a story. Kind of like what Springsteen does, but only worse. Come on, Bruce is the best. With the aid of my Mr. Magoo glasses, I would print my lyrics on a page with a pen. Then, when Patty got home, I would have her put them into my iPad. I wrote songs about everything. I wrote songs about my mother and father. I wrote songs about how angry I was about being fired. I wrote songs about people who once were my friends now did not keep in contact with me anymore. It became my passion. If I heard a phrase, then that phrase would be the basis of a new song.

This was much better than doing an audio diary. This was something that I was very proud of. I am not the most skilled person when it comes to any type of repair, but I was able to express my feelings in a song.

With each passing day, my vision was getting much worse. So I scratched the pen and picked up a marker. This allowed me to see what I was putting down. When I could not write in a straight line, I would put a ruler across the page to use that as my level. I was on fire and nothing could stop me. When I completely lost my vision, I would lie in bed and memorize the song and then have Patty put it on my iPad. By the end of the day I was so exhausted that it was easy for me to fall asleep. My daughter applied a guitar to my lyrics and my sons added their voices. It was really cool to see the whole process come to fruition. I was a songwriter. How about that?

Now what was I going to do with all of these lyrics? Patty searched on the web and we came across what seemed like a reputable songwriting service out of Nashville. They were having a contest and were asking songwriters to send three of their favorite songs. It was free, so I figured what the hell. After about a month, I received an email from the song service saying that

I was not the winner but that they liked one of my song's lyrics. In the email, they said that it would cost X amount of money to have my lyrics put to an acoustic guitar. I love songs with only an acoustic guitar because they are so intimate. Sometimes a song gets lost in all the engineering in the studio, but an acoustic guitar and a voice can't be screwed up. So once again, I said what the hell and we sent a check to the song service. About a month later, I received an email with the MP3 of my song. It was awesome. I was so happy that it turned out great. I even had thoughts of what I was going to say when I won a Grammy for best New Song of the Year.

However, nothing is as good as it seems--just like how Ellio's pizza looks on the box. I have eaten so many of them and they never look like that when they come out of the oven. The woman whom I was communicating with over email, told me that they would take my song and send it out to radio stations. Like a schmuck that I was at the time, I believed her. When I replied to her emails, she would ignore them. When I called the phone number that was attached to the email, it went straight to voicemail. It was a hoax. She got me. Guess what I did? I wrote a song about her. It's really bad ass too. That was my only option, to write a song.

About five years later, I was talking to an old friend of mine from my old job. I found out that he writes lyrics too and we sent lyrics back-and-forth to one another to review. When I sent the lyrics to the song about that bitch from the song service, he told me that he had been snookered by her as well. That's OK, when I went a Pulitzer Prize for this book, I will reveal her name.

Chapter 17 - How Do You Tie Your Shoelaces?

My first recollection of when I performed in public was when I was in fifth grade at St Anastasia's school. I was in a school play in the cafeteria, and I played Pontius Pilate. I wore a robe, washed my hands, and dried my hands. I was amazing. I still can't believe I did not win an Oscar for that performance. OK, I basically was in a play for one minute. The next time was when I was 12 years old and I was dressed in that ridiculous suit jacket that my mom probably bought from a circus clown. I did a reading at my sister's wedding and everyone was laughing at me because my suit jacket looked like my mom opened up a box of crayons and ran an iron over it.

Ever since that day, I couldn't speak in public for quite a while. I probably was traumatized by the whole experience. I took a public-speaking class in college and was terrified when it was my turn to speak in front of the class. I started to speak, but I was out of breath and my voice was shaky. Everyone in the classroom could probably notice that I was sweating. There was a college radio station so I decided to be a disc jockey. That wasn't so bad because no one would see me. I could act all crazy and not be judged by the people looking at me. I was a DJ at a radio station in West Chester. They played 50's music and Patty would go with me to the station early on Saturday and Sunday mornings. She would sit in the recording studio and there was a window between the recording studio and the place where I sat to do my magic. When a song was done, I would turn on the mic and say a joke. When I was done, I would turn off the mic and another song would be playing. I was so proud of myself because I was so funny. Then I would look in the window to the recording studio and see Patty asleep. Great. The only person that is listening to me was falling asleep.

That gave me a lot of confidence. The radio station's signal was so weak that you could barely pick it up in the lobby. After about a year and a half, I called it quits. I was not going to be a radio DJ. If I couldn't make my girlfriend laugh, then I couldn't make anybody else laugh.

When I started to go to the Center, my social worker mentioned that they were looking for clients to go out into the public and speak about their experiences with vision loss. They needed people to go to churches, nursing homes, and schools to educate the public on being blind or visually impaired. I have five nieces and would always joke around with them whenever I saw them at family gatherings. So I mentioned to my social worker that I would be interested in going into schools to talk about my vision loss. When the day arrived, I was picked up by a driver from the Center, along with two friends from the Center. We were taken to a local college to speak to a class of freshmen. This brought me back to when I was a student in college and could barely speak in front of a group of people, and now I was supposed to speak in front of a group of college students, but this time I was blind. However, I really wasn't that nervous. I did not have to see people looking at me. I could just stand in front of them and speak like I was the only person in the room. I talked about my blindness and added some humor to it because that's what you have to do in order to keep your sanity. I talked about how I had gone to a Stevie Wonder concert the night before and that I wasn't the only blind person in the arena. This isn't a joke. I did go to the Stevie Wonder concert the night before. One of the students asked me if I experienced a concert differently now that I could not see. I never thought of that before, but I told him that I was noticing each instrument differently. Whereas before, I would hear all the instruments at once, this time I could pick out one instrument at a time and just listen to it. In one song I would listen to the bass part, and then the next song I would listen to the drums, and so on and so on.

The next time we went out to speak, it was to a group of fourth graders. We sat in front of the library and the students would come in to the library, 50 at a time. We talked for five different sessions and by the end of the day we were all punch drunk. It was so enjoyable for me because the fourth-grade students were so attentive and asked so many questions. They asked us how we knew what clothes we were wearing and they asked the two ladies with me how they put on their make-up. I told them that it is easy for me to get dressed in the morning because I just put on a T-shirt, sweatshirt, and a pair of jeans. However, it is much more difficult for a woman because they have to put on make-up. The two ladies with me told the students that they put a pin in their shirt a certain way to notify them what color the shirt is. I never thought of it that way, but it is brilliant.

The next time we spoke in front of a group of fourth graders in a gymnasium. They were all sitting on the floor of the basketball court in front of us. Before we started our talk though, one of the teachers told us that there was a blind student in the school. He came into the gymnasium with his small walkingstick and it broke my heart. What a brave boy he was. The great thing about it was that every student knew him and they treated him with kindness. They helped him out in any way. I found out later that this type of treatment is not given to adults. We should learn from children because they show the most empathy for those who are in need. The social worker started out our meeting by asking for volunteers to come up and put on glasses that show what your vision is like, depending on your disease. For instance, glasses that show what it looks like to have diabetic retinopathy. Glasses that show what it looks like to have glaucoma. Glasses that show what it looks like to have cataracts. Finally, she would bring one student up and blindfold them, spin them around, and then ask them where the other students were. This was showing the student what it was like to be blind. When the student would point, the other students would get a kick out of where the student pointed because it was never at them.

One of the ladies would talk about her walking cane and how she uses it in public. She would tell them how she would go for a walk around her apartment complex every day with the aid of her cane. Then she would ask for a volunteer to come up and she would show them the proper way to approach a person walking with a cane. She would tell them that you should never grab the arm of a blind person when they are walking because you will startle them. What you should do is allow that blind person to grab onto your arm. At that point, she would have the volunteer close their eyes and see what it would be like to walk with a walking stick.

Next, my other friend at the Center would show them how blind people use an iPhone. For instance, how we can text, email, or phone a family member or anyone else just by voice command. She would show them an application on her phone that is called Be My Eyes that is used whenever a blind person needs help. All you have to do is click on the application and someone anywhere in the world will answer it and they will see your video screen and what you were looking at and they will help you to find or read your mail or instructions on a box to cook dinner. She would show them how the iPhone has an application that allows you to read what denomination paper currency is. I would talk about what it was like to show empathy for those who are visually impaired, or have any other disability. I recall when I was around 14 years old, I rode my bike up to the 7-11 store in Newtown Square to get a Slurpee. As I was leaving the store, there was a woman who was trying to help her husband out the back of her van. He was in a wheelchair and the back of the van had a hydraulic lift to aid him. When she saw me, she asked if I could help her out. I didn't even think twice about it. When I was done helping them, they both thanked me. I thought that was the proper thing to do. Why wouldn't anyone help them in that situation? I wondered afterward if the reason why they thanked me was because not many people in my situation would have done that.

Maybe it was because my sister was born mentally impaired. I guess that's where I knew what it was like to show empathy. I knew what it was like to have someone be shunned just because of who they were. My brother, sisters, and I always took it upon ourselves to protect my sister from anyone that was being cruel to her. It didn't matter where it happened. I recall my sister getting into a boy's face on the school bus because he was being mean to my impaired sister. She was going to punch him in the nose because he was teasing her. To this day, I can't stand a bully. Bullies pick on others who are weaker but when you stand-up to a bully, that's when they back down and show their true worth.

My parents never asked that we protect our sister. We just did it because she was family and that's what families do. I got into many a fight with my friends whenever they made comments about my sister. It didn't matter how big they were, they were going to get it from me. Once again, they were picking on someone who was different from them. Maybe they picked up this attitude from their parents.

When my sister was younger, she had a lot of friends in the neighborhood. As she got older, she would go to their homes and knock on their doors to see if they wanted to play. Most of the time however, she would come home upset because they would say no. I'm sure this broke my mom and dad's hearts to see my sister upset. Now if these kids had good parents, their parents would tell their children to go out and play with her because they are no better than she was. They didn't though, and that's a shame. I know I raised my kids to accept others for who they are and I know that my sisters and brother taught their children the same lesson.

My sister loved to play cards and her favorite game was Crazy Eights. I remember one time when I was around 12 years old, I came home and my dad wanted me to play cards with her. Being a little shit that I was, I told him that I didn't want to. As you recall, my dad never really had to say anything to me to get his point across. His favorite motto was "actions speak louder than words". His actions spoke plenty to me when I said no. He just gave me the steely blue eyes and I melted. I relented and I played cards with her. Now, I wasn't being that way because my sister was mentally impaired, I was just being a typical brother to his sister.

As each of my sisters got married and moved out of the house, my sister's impairment got worse. I believe that she was well aware of what was going on with her and that she would never lead a normal life like her siblings. This definitely took a toll on my mom and dad's marriage. How could it not? How could they not look at other families in our neighborhood who did not have a disabled child and not feel resentful toward God. There was many a night when my mother would lie in her bed and say the rosary. I imagine that she was praying to God for my sister to get better or for the strength to deal with her changing moods. She relied on her faith to get her through much of the adversity in her life.

When I was 12 years old, I went to New York City with my mom, dad, and sister. She was going to have a surgery to hopefully help her speak better. In the car ride up, my mom and dad had so much hope that this surgery would improve her speech and allow her to live a more resourceful life. However, it didn't turn out the way they had planned. This was devastating news to them, but more devastating to my sister. She went downhill very quickly after that. She became very angry, and I don't blame her. That's why I hate the expression, "everything happens for a reason". Really? What reason was it for my sister and I have to live like this? The only conclusion is free will. That's the only reason. Nothing more than that. It wasn't God's fault, although I'm sure my mom and dad got mad at him or her for that. I know that my sisters, brother and I did.

I was 18 years old when my brother got married and moved out of the house. It was just my mom, dad, sister, and me. I believe that's when my sister was at her worst. She became less and less communicative and more and more explosive with my mom and dad. Everything that they tried, did not make it better. I could see in their eyes how despondent they were with the whole situation. I don't know how they did it, but they did. They were two very strong, Italian people. I can't imagine what it was like for them to have to go through that.

When I got married at 23 and left the house, it was just my mom, dad and my sister. I'm sure that they were thinking about their own mortality and who would care for her when they were gone. That was probably their thought as soon as they found out that my sister was mentally impaired. Well, that day finally arrived. They needed to place my sister in a home where she would get the proper care and attention that she so dearly needed. Thankfully, my sisters and brother found a communal living arrangement right up the road from my mom and dad's old Cape Cod home. My sister thrived in that environment and she was very happy. That put all our minds at ease knowing that she would be taken care of for the rest of her life. My mom and dad could visit her whenever they wanted, and deliver her favorite beverage: coffee. My sister loves coffee. When my mom would brew a pot of coffee, my sister's eyes were bulging out of her head. My mom and dad would take her on a drive to Dairy Queen for an ice cream or just to drive around Newtown Square. It was a peaceful car ride for the three of them. She would sit in the back drinking her coffee and have a big smile on her face. How simplistic their lives had become. Where once there was anger and sadness, now there was a pleasant existence for all of them.

Each Christmas, the community living home would have a Christmas party and all the family would show up. My sister enjoyed this so much because she was the center of attention, as she should be. When my sister was younger, she didn't like any physical affection , but now when we greeted her, she would allow us to hug her and she would put her head on our chest. I thought that was so adorable. Then she would sit next to us and hold our hand the whole time. This was something that she never would have done when she was living at home. I know that this made my mom and dad very happy because my sister was happy and that was all that mattered to all of us. Her happiness was first and foremost in all of our minds. When it was time to go, she would give all of us a hug and then she would go into her room. Sad to think that was her life, but it was.

When my mom and dad moved into an assisted living home, it was an hour and a half away from Newtown Square, so they never saw my sister again. It was too much for my sisters or brother to take my mom and dad to my sister's home because of their worsening condition. It would also have been too much for my sister to visit my mom and dad in the assisted living home. My parents would call her to see how she was doing, but at that point she only really said a few words. I'm sure that this was devastating to both my parents, but they were at peace knowing that she was going to be OK. When my mother was told that she would be moving from the assisted living part of the nursing home to the skilled nursing part, she got very upset and wanted to know if her daughter would be OK. That was first and foremost in her mind. My sister was always first and foremost in my parents' minds. They knew that we would be fine, so they didn't worry about us. My sisters, brother, Patty and I would visit her and take her out for a drive. We would never forget her favorite beverage of course. When Patty and I took her out for a drive, I would sit in the back seat and hold her hand and talk to her. She would laugh when Patty would say that I was ugly. After about a 30-minute drive around the area, Patty would pull in the driveway to my sister's home. She would quickly open up the door and start to run inside without saying goodbye. Patty and I would tell her to stop, and she would come back and give us both a hug with her head pressed against our chest. How sweet that was.

So I think I had a pretty good definition of what the word empathy meant. I had seen people who showed empathy to my sister and people who had not. I had heard the stories of my friends at the Center and how they were either shown empathy or not. I could also rely on my thoughts on the matter since losing my vision. What a better audience to talk about empathy then with fourth graders. My daughter teaches fourth grade and I know how much she not only teaches them about science, math, social studies and other subjects, but on how to treat others with respect. This is the best time to teach young children about empathy. It's just like teaching a two-year-old how to swim or how to ski. You do it when they are young so they do not have the fear. You show children empathy when they are young, and when they get older it will be a natural reaction.

So when I stood up to speak in front of the kids, I would ask an unsuspecting volunteer to come up. Of course they had no idea what they were in for. I would ask them what their favorite song was and when they told me what it was, I would tell them to sing it for me. They got so embarrassed and the rest of the students laughed. Sometimes I would ask them what their favorite movie was and then have them tell me their favorite line. Ultimately, they would be all nervous and forget what to say. One time before I spoke, I asked the students if they could give me a standing ovation and they obliged. Another time, I had written five different introductions that a student read out loud and just like a comedian working-out his stuff in a smoke-filled basement of a comedy store, my introductions did not get a laugh and they bombed badly. This would loosen up the kids and let them know that I was not there to lecture them, but to have a good time and let them know what it's like to not have vision. I remember a lot of times in middle school and high school where they had someone come to speak to the kids in the auditorium and it got to be pretty boring. I did not want these kids to be bored but entertained and also not to be afraid of someone who was blind. That we are just like them but we just can't see.

The students asked us if we dream. Now, I never knew this before, but people who have been blind from birth do not see anything in their dreams. They can hear but they can't see. It's almost like listening to a radio. Since the woman and I had vision before we lost it, we could see in our dreams. I used to golf a lot in my 20s. My friends and I from work would take the northeast extension of the turnpike until it ended at a golf resort in Tunkhannock, Pennsylvania. So when I started to lose my vision, I would dream about golfing. I golfed just as bad in my dreams as I did when I actually played golf. The part that made it frustrating for me in my dreams, is that my friends and I were carrying our bags but I could not keep up with them. It's like I was walking in quicksand. What I got from that, is that they were moving on with their lives and leaving me behind. I still dream about going to work, but in my dreams it's not the building that I worked at. I will dream about people who I worked with and when I get to my desk, someone else is sitting there.

I once spoke in front of eight or nine Girl Scouts at a local church with this other guy from the Center. We were sitting at a table with the Girl Scouts and this one girl was sitting off to my left, about 3 feet away from me, when I started to speak. By the time I was done, the social worker who was with us told me that she was sitting real close to me. It's like at first she didn't know how to react to me but then she loosened up. I got a kick out of that. The guy that was with me was a runner and he showed the girls the harness that he uses to attach himself to another runner. He runs in marathons and I thought that was really neat.

I spoke at a local YMCA during the summer and the kids came in straight from the pool in their bathing suits with towels wrapped around them. I figured it would be more intimate if I sat down on the gymnasium floor with them when I spoke. I felt like Gene London or Captain Kangaroo or Captain Noah. I told them that you should not only show empathy to those who are disabled, but also to their classmates when they are having a hard time. One day, you will be having a difficult day and you will need someone to show empathy to you. The kids were great. I would ask them what the word empathy and compassion meant and they knew right away.

The best part of speaking in front of students, was when it was their turn to ask questions. They came up with such great questions too. I was once asked how I shave, and I told them with a razor and shaving cream. My favorite all-time question was, how do you tie your shoelaces? My answer? Just like you do. I would tell the person who asked me, to close their eyes and untie their shoes and then tie them. Then I would tell them that's how I time my shoes. I once told a student that I could guess what he was wearing and what he looked like. I told him that he had short hair, and he replied yes. I told him that he was wearing a T-shirt and he said yes. I told him that he was wearing shorts and he said yes. I told him that he was wearing socks and he said yes. I told him that he was wearing sneakers and he said yes. By this time, he was perplexed. He actually thought I could see what he was wearing, when in actuality I was just guessing because it was summertime and I knew more than likely that his hair would be short and he be wearing a T-shirt and shorts. The kid thought I was the amazing Kreskin or Chriss Angel.

Hopefully the students got as much out of our discussions with them as I did. I thoroughly enjoyed every time we went out. You just never knew what to expect when the kids were asked if they had any questions. After one meeting at a local school, the kids wrote thank-you cards to us. One of the students who thanked me, drew a picture of me on the front of the card. Patty told me that it was hysterical because my nostrils look like they were 5 feet wide. I figured that the student's perspective of me was from below and that's all he could see.

These students are probably in high school by now. My only wish for them is that when they encounter someone who is not only blind, but disabled like my sister, they will show them empathy. The days when their friends are feeling down, I sure hope that they are there to show compassion because there will be a time when they will be down or despondent and they will need a friend to listen and pick them up. It's actually a great lesson for anyone of any age. We are not too old to start learning. So when you come across somebody who is blind, ask them if they need help and allow them to hold your arm. If you come across someone who is trying to help their disabled child or husband or mother out of a van, stop and help them. Finally, please have empathy for those who are less fortunate than us, like my sister. You may think that this will never happen to you, just like I did, but adversity finds all of us. Now it is my time to get off the soapbox, I sure hope I don't fall down.

I decided that I wanted to join the Center's trivia group once a month. I was never much of a book reader when I was younger and also was not a great student. When I lost my vision, I started to listen to audible books. I got very interested in history. History about World War I, World War II, and the Civil War. This opened up my mind to other subjects besides sports and entertainment. To show you a devious side of me, I also liked reading books about serial killers. Don't ask me why but I do.

I was always that guy that sucked at Trivial Pursuit. I would have at least two pieces in my wheel and those two subjects would be entertainment and sports. I was horrible at literature, history, geography, and science. After reading many history books, I was not as embarrassed to play Trivial Pursuit at the Center. There was one guy who is part of our low-vision group that I never really got to know very well because I didn't sit near him during the meetings. I knew that he was into sports and I asked him if they needed any other players on his team for Trivial Pursuit. I'm glad that I asked him because I got to know him much better and he is one of my best friends. We had a great time playing. It got to be very competitive with the other team and I looked forward to playing each month. We would tease each other if we got an answer wrong but it never got too serious where anybody's feelings were hurt.

I came up with an idea that I thought people at the Center would enjoy. I would ask a client five questions so that other clients would get to know them better. These were not deep questions by any means, but they were goofy questions that would let other people get to know a different side of that person. My first attempt was with my buddy from the Trivial Pursuit and low-vision group. The first question that I asked him was "Ginger or

Marianne?" At this point, he knew me a little bit from the Trivial group but not enough to know that I would ask him that question. He was caught off guard and then he told me that I was just as messed up in the head as he was. I knew that we would get along just fine. His answer was Marianne by the way. That was the correct answer.

From that point, I interviewed 15 more people at the center and everyone had a great time. Then I decided that I wanted to do a game show with the group. My first thought was Family Feud. My three sisters, aunt, and I tried out for the Family Feud when Richard Dawson was the host, but we were not selected. When the show was brought back with a different host, we tried out again and this time we got accepted. However, they canceled the show before we ever got a chance to appear. I guess it was not in the cards for us.

When I brought up Family Feud at the Center, everyone thought it would be a great idea. The second game that I added was the Match Game. I love this game because it was so raunchy back in the mid to late 70s. Gene Rayburn used a microphone that looked like a drumstick. I came up with the questions for both games and was actually thinking about going to a thrift store and wearing an ugly suit jacket. Hell, I was even thinking about wearing that ridiculous looking "Joseph and the multicolored dream coat" jacket. Why not, most of the people wouldn't be able to see what kind of jacket I was wearing so I would be free of ridicule.

Everyone had a good time with the games and it became a success. So much so, that it became the event that everybody wanted to attend. I got to be my normal self, which is extremely scary, and people got to know the real me. For an hour one day a month, I got to pretend that I was Richard Dawson, but I did not kiss anybody like he did. That would be wrong.

There is an old photo of a bunch of construction workers sitting on a steel beam and eating lunch. They have their steel lunch pails next to them, and they have to be at least 500 feet up in the air. Every time I saw that photo, it would give me the chills. How brave those men were. Then I would think, how would I react in that situation, and I think I would be scared shitless. Just thinking about that photo now, makes me a little insane. To them, it was nothing. It was just another day at work. I would imagine them getting up when their lunch was done and walking across the steel beam back to begin their afternoon.

I worked for a painting company for a little bit when I was in my early 20s and I had to paint the outside windows that were on the second floor. I grabbed the extension ladder and I extended it up just below the windowsills and looked up at how high I would be. After a few minutes of thought, I walked inside and climbed the stairs into the bedroom where the extension ladder was leaning against. I opened the window and leaned out as far as I could, and painted the exterior of the windows. There was no way in hell that I was going to risk my life climbing up that extension ladder and having my knees rattle back-and-forth and then have the paint fall down in the garden below, not to mention that I was probably getting paid a little bit above minimum wage.

When the guy that I was with came back to the house, he asked me what the hell I was doing. I told him that I was afraid of heights and I thought I would do a better job if I leaned out the window instead of climbing the ladder. Needless to say, I didn't last very long at that painting company. I think that if I had to work on a high-rise project and eat my lunch sitting on a steel beam with the city below me, I don't think I ever would've come home with a dry pair of underwear.

Even Superman was afraid of heights. Well, not Clark Kent, but my dad. Yup. My bad-ass father was afraid of heights. The favorite story I ever heard my mom tell me about my dad, was when they were in Paris and they went to the top of the Eiffel Tower. My mom was fearless. I can't think of any time that she was afraid. So she went to the edge of the viewing deck and my dad sat along the interior. My mom looked over her shoulder and told my dad, "come over here with me". Superman says, "hell no, Catherine". Good man. That's not enough for my mom. Here is my dad, terrified of heights but that doesn't stop my mom. She said to him, "if you love me then you will come over here". My dad had the greatest comeback ever. He told her, "then I don't love you". How awesome is that?

Fast forward to 2002 and Patty and I are celebrating our 15th wedding anniversary in Las Vegas. There is a casino on the strip that's called Paris. They have a replica of the Eiffel Tower, but it is half the size of the real one. The Eiffel Tower is 1000 feet, and the tower in Las Vegas is 500 feet. So of course Patty wants to go up to the top of the tower but I am hesitant because as you know by now, I am terrified of heights. It's actually not the fear of heights but it's the fear of falling that gets me the most. Anyway, we take the elevator all the way to the top, and as the elevator doors open Patty proceeds to go to the edge and I lean up against the interior wall. Just like my dad did in Paris, I am doing the same thing in Las Vegas. The only difference was that Patty did not tell me to come to the edge. She knew better than to say that to me. Now the tower that I was standing on in Las Vegas was half the size of what my dad had to encounter in Paris that night. I was overlooking Sin City, not the City of Lights. I think my dad was brave just to go all the way to the top. I really don't believe I would've done that. Hell, I didn't even want to go to the top of the Cape May Lighthouse.

I went to Cincinnati, Ohio for a business trip with two other people from my office. Our hotel was in Covington, Kentucky, which is across the Ohio River from Cincinnati. One night after work, we went back to our hotel and decided to go see a baseball game at Riverfront Stadium. We took a taxi to the ballpark and after the game the two people that were with me decided it would be a good idea to walk back to our hotel. I didn't think too much about it. I didn't think about having to walk over a bridge. It never crossed my mind that that's how we would have to get back to our hotel. Stupid me.

So we approached the bridge and had to climb two flights of stairs to get to the top. This was one of those old bridges that had a sidewalk on the outer part of the bridge. Each time a car would drive by, the bridge would rattle. We started to walk across the bridge and all of a sudden my knees locked. I was so scared. I was walking like Frankenstein's monster. One woman was walking with me and tried to calm me down. That didn't help because I could hear the Ohio River below me and it was calling my name. The woman behind us was about 10 feet away and she had no idea that I was freaking-out. It's crazy to have the fear of heights, but I almost wanted to jump off of the bridge to end that fear. After what seemed like an hour, which probably was 10 minutes, we got to the other end of the bridge. I was never so happy to be in Kentucky. I got down on my hands and knees and kissed the ground. I had survived.

On a crisp fall day in November, 2000, Patty, the kids, and I went to see the Statue of Liberty. Patty is the Statue of Liberty's favorite fan. She actually has a shelf in our house with replicas of the Statue of Liberty. On this particular morning, as we waited for the ferry to take us to Liberty Island, the sky was foggy and you could barely see New York City across the harbor. Before we could get on the boat, we waited for the fog to dissipate. After about 30 minutes, the World Trade Center towers appeared, looming high above lower Manhattan. I had never seen them up close and it took my breath away. I thought of those men who were sitting on the steel beams high above New York City eating their lunch and how they probably built that building.

When we arrived on Liberty Island, Lady Liberty was awaiting our arrival to the top of her crown. The first flight of stairs was just like walking up a flight of stairs in a regular building until you got into the exterior of the statue. This is where my nightmare began. You had to go up a spiral staircase to the top of the Statue of Liberty. I did not know this beforehand. Probably something I should've known or found out before we did this adventure. As we started our climb, my knees started to shake. The sides of the stairs were probably only up to my abdomen. I wish it was all the way up to my head. Patty, Emily, and Kevin were in front of Bryan and me. Kevin has no fear of heights and neither does Patty. Emily was a little uneasy but she was doing much better than Bryan and I. As we got halfway up the stairs, I was climbing them on my knees and so was Bryan. Kevin was completely oblivious to the fact that Bryan and I are probably peeing our underwear and he said out loud to me, "hey dad, look how high up we are!" At which point I replied, "shut the hell up, Kevin!" I know I'm not going to win any father-of-the-year awards.

Finally we got to the top and I was relieved, but Bryan was not. There are four or five holes in the statue's crown that you can look through to the harbor in New York City. I had no problem with that because they were at eye level and it was not that large of a hole that made me feel like I was going to fall. Not Bryan though. No more than 10 seconds after getting to the top, Bryan replied, "OK, let's go down now". That's my boy.

The view was absolutely breathtaking. I can still remember looking at those two towers high above the other buildings. Sadly though, those two buildings would be hit by two airplanes 10 months later and forever change all our lives. Going down the stairs was a breeze for me. I had no issues or fear whatsoever because I knew that I was going down instead of going up. There was a woman in front of me who was going down the stairs on her butt. She was crying out loud. I felt so bad for her because that's how I was feeling when going up.

Patty, the kids and I went on a vacation to North Carolina. In the movie Forrest Gump, Tom Hanks' character runs back and forth across the United States. One of the mountains that he runs up, is Grandfather Mountain in North Carolina. On every vacation, Patty always wants to go to the top of a mountain. Does she realize that I am scared of heights? Anyway, we drove to the top of Grandfather Mountain. To get to the tallest part, you have to walk across a bridge. Now this isn't just any bridge. It's a narrow, walking suspension bridge. Now there is no way in hell that I was going to cross this bridge. So I waved goodbye to Patty and the kids and I waited for them to cross and come back. This old woman was sitting next to me and she told me that she was afraid of heights and that she was not going over the bridge. She and I bonded over our fear of heights. Here I am, a 45-year-old man commiserating with an 85-year-old grandmother. Such is life. Was I emasculated by all of this? Hell no! A good friend of mine, who was also afraid of heights, once told me that he didn't care if people gave him a hard time about not going up to the top of buildings or mountains. That's how I felt. Who cares if there were six-year-old kids that were laughing at me for not walking over the bridge.

Why did I tell you all the stories about my encounters with fear of heights? I'm glad you asked. You didn't ask? I'm going to tell you anyway. My good friend at the Center brought up the idea of skydiving. At first I thought she was joking. Me, skydiving? Are you kidding me? Remember how I couldn't go higher than two steps on the grandstands at our football stadium when I was a little kid? Now you expect me to skydive? However, the longer I thought about it, the cooler the idea sounded

We talked about going skydiving on the same day, but our schedules did not line up. She eventually went skydiving in May 2015 in New Jersey, and I scheduled my skydive in July in Upper Bucks County, Pennsylvania.

The trip to the Perkasie airport took an hour from our home. The morning was hot, hazy, and humid, which is usually the weather in the summertime in southeastern Pennsylvania. When we arrived, we watched a training video which showed the proper form to use when jumping out of a plane. It showed how to bend your arms at the elbows and spread them out to the side, arch your torso and bend your legs with your heels touching your ass. After that, Patty and I went outside to meet my tandem-jumping buddy. He was a really cool, Australian man. He had never tandem jumped with a blind person before so I was his first. We again went over the proper techniques when jumping out of a plane, and then he had me put on my harness. We sat and talked a little bit before the plane arrived. There was another jumper with him who was going to videotape the whole experience. My buddy attached himself to my harness and as the plane arrived, we walked to the airplane. There were about 10 other jumpers with us and the plane was not too big.

We were going to be the first ones to jump out of the plane, so we sat next to the door on the right side. As the plane took off, I was surprised to find out that they never shut the door.

The jumper that was going to videotape my skydive, sat across from us and filmed me as we took off. As the plane approached 13,000 feet, my Australian buddy, leaned forward and asked me if I was still good to go. This must have looked pretty funny because I literally was sitting on his lap like a ventriloquist dummy. I told him that I was all good to go and then a minute later he tapped me on my shoulder to stand up. The inside of the plane was so loud that you could barely hear anyone speak. As we walked to the open door, we looked like two men who had escaped a chain gang. The jumper who was going to videotape my adventure, went to the door and jumped out and grabbed onto the outside of the plane. My Australian buddy and I then slowly walked to the open door. There were handles on either side of the door and we stood there awaiting our cue to jump. Everything leading up to this point had been peaceful to me. However, this is where my fear came out of my body, and as I was standing on the edge ready to jump, I said to myself, oh shit, I'm really going to do this. At that point, my tandem buddy tapped me on the shoulder and counted backwards from three. As he hit one, all the training that was told to me by him and in that video disappeared. We took off in a freefall and the wind was incredible. It hit me so powerfully that I couldn't breathe. I started to freak out a little bit, shaking my head back-and-forth. I bent my knees back towards my butt and put my arms wide out in front of me. Little did I know that I was being videotaped by the jumper who was right in front of us. After about 10 seconds, I caught my breath and started to enjoy the dive. I started to wave towards the camera and give a thumbs up and then the middle finger

Even though I was free falling from 13,000 feet at about 120 miles an hour, it didn't feel like I was falling. It felt like I was stationary and the wind was coming up below me and holding me in place. This must have been the one thousandth time that my Australian guide had jumped, but he was screaming and enjoying it like it was his first. I joined in and it was awesome. As we approached land, he pulled up on the parachute string and we abruptly arched upward. That feeling of recklessness disappeared. As fast as that rush had been jumping out of the plane, that's how quick the serenity of the whole experience appeared. What a juxtaposition. Jumping at 120 miles an hour and then floating like a feather.

My Australian buddy allowed me to pull the guide strings to the left and right, and we floated down like an eagle. As we neared the ground, he told me to put my legs out in front of me like I was sitting in mid air, and then we landed as soft as landing on a bed, as my butt hit the ground. It was absolutely incredible. The most intense and amazing experience in my life. It was such a rush. Something that I never would have done if I could see. From the time we jumped from the plane until we hit the ground was only 60 seconds.

We brought the video tape of the skydive to my sister's house. My whole family screamed as they saw me approach the plane. They screamed louder as I approached the open door. Then they absolutely freaked- out when I jumped. It was like they were in the plane with me. They told me that I was nuts. Maybe I was. I was living my life though. I wasn't sitting on the couch wallowing in my self-pity. I was taking risks--controlled risks.

My whole life I was so afraid of heights. and I never tried to overcome that fear. I allowed that fear to take control of me. Now that I couldn't see, I took on that fear and I beat its ass. I want to skydive again one day. It's a feeling that cannot be matched by any other adventure. Patty, Bryan, and I went zip lining in the Poconos later that summer, and that was exciting but not even close to skydiving. George H. W. Bush went sky diving on his 80th and then 90th birthday's. If I am still alive, I want to do the same.

Chapter 19 - Mile High Club

There is a great song by Johnny Cash called, "I've Been Everywhere". It
goes as follows:

I've been to:

Boston, Charleston, Dayton, Louisiana,

Washington, Houston, Kingston, Texarkana,

Monterey, Faraday, Santa Fe, Tallapoosa,

Glen Rock, Black Rock, Little Rock, Oskaloosa,

Tennessee to Tennessee Chicopee, Spirit Lake,

Grand Lake, Devils Lake, Crater Lake, for Pete's sake.

I'd been to only one of those places, and that was Boston. Patty, the kids,
and I went on vacation in 2008 and in 2012 to get my retina checked-out
by a world-renowned uveitis doctor. So when Patty mentioned that she
wanted to go to San Francisco, I was a bit hesitant to say the least.
Thinking of sitting on a plane for 5 1/2 hours, completely blind, scared me
a little bit. I didn't know if I would be able to handle the flight, let alone go
to a place where I had wanted to visit my whole life. I was always
enamored with San Francisco, Lombard Street, Golden Gate Bridge, and
not to mention Alcatraz. How would I handle being there and not being
able to see the famous landmarks? Would that put me into a permanent
downward spiral?

With constant persistence though, I relented and Patty planned a vacation.
Patty loves planning vacations. She setup an Excel spreadsheet in different
colors which included we were going to eat lunch and dinner and at what

time. It's like going on a vacation with a drill sergeant. In March 2014, we drove to Philadelphia International Airport for our flight to the *city by the bay*. It was so weird for me. I was holding onto Patty's arm with one hand, the walking cane in my other hand, while she wheeled our suitcases through the terminal. I felt so vulnerable and I had to put all my trust in Patty. That was difficult for me to do. We went through the TSA baggage check and when Patty let go of my arm for me to go through the metal detector, I felt a little uneasy. Just letting go of her arm made me feel uncomfortable because she was my security blanket. Once we got through, I started to relax. Waiting at the terminal gate for our flight was much different than five years ago when awaiting our flight to Denver. This time I was much more relaxed and not so much in a panic. I had prepared myself for what it would be like in a plane without my vision… just like a football coach preparing a game plan against a bitter rival.

When we got on the plane, Patty sat in the middle seat and I sat in the aisle seat. As I would realize with every trip after this, nothing would ever be easy. Before I sat down, I banged my head into the overhead compartment. That pissed me off so much. Something that I once did with ease and didn't have to think about, now I would have to take my time. As the flight entered its third hour, I put on music from my iPad. Ironically, the first song that came on was Lights, by Journey. The song says the following lines: "I want to get back to my city by the bay". Well, I wasn't going back to the city by the bay, but what an appropriate song at that moment. I took off one headphone and tapped Patty on the arm to put it onto her ear. I think that was my way of telling Patty that I would be OK on the trip.

Patty loves to stay at old hotels. So we stayed at the Fairmont in San Francisco. It was a beautiful hotel. In hindsight though, we probably should have done a lot of walking to prepare for our trip to San Francisco because that city is so damn hilly. One night after eating dinner, we thought that we could walk back to our hotel without taking the cable car. Wrong idea. Halfway up this half -mile hill, that was probably at a 30° angle, Patty and I both stopped and put our hands on our knees. Huffing and puffing, we waited there for about five minutes before we went up about another 30 steps and did the same.

We took a boat to Alcatraz where they had an audible tour so I could listen to a tape describing how the bird man and his fellow inmates escaped. We overlooked the courtyard where the inmates spent an hour each day. I had seen so many images of Alcatraz over the years, that I just let my imagination run wild. Thinking of how that little island had a view of San Francisco. How the city looks so close, but it was so far.

We walked through Chinatown and this is where I let my nose take over for my eyes. I knew that I was in Chinatown just buy the scent of the food that was being cooked. Not to mention the music that was playing, which is where my ears came into play. I had to rely on my other senses in order for me to enjoy the vacation. Of course, what would a stroll through Chinatown be without me falling on the sidewalk. Yup, that's exactly what happened. I was on the sidewalk, close to the street, when I turned my ankle on the curb. I proceeded to fall face-first on the ground, but luckily my pretty face was not injured because I had placed my hands down in front of me just in the nick of time.

Ninety-nine percent of the time, the citizens of San Francisco were so kind to Patty and me--always looking out for us. One time we were waiting at a cable car stop with about 20 people. When it arrived, it was filled to capacity and normally would have bypassed our stop. However, it stopped abruptly and opened its door. People started to walk towards the cable car, but the operator motioned them off and told us to get on board. How kind was that?

The one incident of rudeness happened when Patty and I were at Pier 39. We were standing at a window watching a guy make a turtle out of sour dough. While standing there, I had my cane in front of me. Some asshole then decided to walk in front of me instead of walking around me . She bumped me and then proceeded to walk over my cane. What a fucking asshole. I swung my cane trying to hit her but I missed.

In 2011, I started to hear a ringing in my ear. We went to see an ear, nose, and throat specialist and he told me that I had tinnitus. This disease is not curable. The doctor had to be one of the strangest doctors I ever met in my 20 years. He was a little guy, and when he came into the room, he stood about as far away as possible. We determined that he either was a germaphobe, had OCD, or was just a complete whack job. I went with the latter, but Patty went with the former. He wanted me to get an MRI of my brain. What is up with these doctors wanting to get an MRI of my brain? It was already determined that I had one. Anyway, when we went back to his office for the test results, he told me that he thought that I had MS because he saw a spot on the right side of my brain. Now, I have been told that I had a lot of things, but when this guy told me that he thought I had MS, I laughed out loud. I told him that you had to be fucking kidding me. We had another MRI performed and it was determined that I did not have that.

For years Patty and the kids were telling me that I needed to get my ears checked. They told me that I was losing my hearing and that I should get hearing aids. I was defiant. There was no way I was going to get my ears checked. I didn't want to have to wear hearing aids and also be blind. However, I relented and I got my hearing checked out. Of course, they were right. I needed hearing aids. I hated wearing them. I still do today.

So here I am on vacation, blind and wearing hearing aids. Patty and I took a trip to Napa Valley with a bunch of ignorant tourists. We stopped at the first vineyard and tasted wine. At the next stop though, these ignorant tourists were talking so loud that I could not hear the lady describing what each bottle of wine was. I leaned towards Patty and told her that I was going to say something. She pleaded with me not to. However, there is this little devil inside of me who told me to tell them to shut the fuck up. So, I listened to the devil. I turned around and said very loudly, would you guys shut the hell up! I can't hear what the woman is saying. Guess what? They did. Afterwards I walked up to the woman from the winery and apologized for my outburst and she actually thanked me for speaking up. When we walked back to the bus, Patty told me to bring my cane the next time so that we wouldn't be beaten up. So I complied, but at the next stop they were quiet.

We rented a car one day to go to see the redwoods. As we drove over the Golden Gate Bridge, I told Patty to let me know when we were on the bridge. She told me that we were on the bridge right now. Much to my amazement, it really was nothing special to drive over.

When we walked through Muir Woods, I was able to feel the huge tree trunks that had been growing for over hundreds of years. It was really amazing. Once again, I let my imagination run wild. I'm not going to lie now…there were times during the vacation, only for a few seconds or minutes, that I would get depressed. Like one time when Patty said that the view was amazing overlooking the city onto the bay. That stopped me in my tracks. However, I bit my upper lip and did not let her know that I was sad. She was great though. She realized what she said and apologized.

We had such a great time and it was good to get out and about in the real world. I had made such giant steps in such a short amount of time. Only a year ago, I didn't want to get out of the house. Now here I was vacationing across the country. I was proud of myself.

When we got back from vacation, everybody at the Center wanted to know how it went. I told them all about it and then said that I had joined the Mile High Club. It was hysterical because my social worker stopped and then said to me, "What did you just say?". I repeated once again that I had joined the Mile High Club. Everybody started to laugh because they knew that I was joking. One sweet woman kept pressing me to describe what that meant. So I reluctantly and embarrassingly told her what it meant. She laughed out loud. So did everyone else. I didn't join the club this trip, it was the following one. Just kidding.

Since our trip to San Francisco went so well, Patty decided that we should go on vacation again. This was fine with me because I knew that I could survive it. In no particular order, we went to the following places: California, Alaska, Hawaii, Arizona, Wyoming, Utah, South Dakota, Nebraska, Oklahoma, Texas, Louisiana, Tennessee, Ohio, Michigan, West Virginia, Kentucky, Mexico, Bahamas, Italy, Montana, Idaho, Maryland, Colorado, Virginia, New York, Washington, Georgia, South Carolina, Indiana, Illinois, Missouri, Vancouver and Virginia. Just like Johnny Cash, I've been everywhere, man or woman. Each trip was unique. Each trip we stayed at old hotels.

On one trip to Arizona, we stopped in Winslow, Arizona. To be precise, I was standing on a corner in Winslow, Arizona. It was such a fine sight to see. I had my girl but she was not in a flatbed Ford. Recognize the song? It's called Take It Easy by the Eagles. Patty planned for us to go to Winslow. This used to be a hotspot before Eisenhower signed a law to make the interstate highways. Winslow was off Route 66. Since the tourists had dried up, they decided to put a statue of Glenn Frey, a girl, a flatbed Ford, and a guitar in a park. There was a speaker in the park that played Eagles music 24 hours a day. What a pleasant surprise that was for me.

Afterwards, we made our way to Flagstaff, Arizona for the night. This was another old, haunted hotel. It was really cool and unique because famous actors had frequented that hotel over the years. So much so, that they had rooms named after them. For instance, Doris Day and Marilyn Monroe. Our room was named after Robert Englund. I laughed out loud when Patty told me that was our room. Patty had no idea who he was. Do you recognize the name? Well, Robert Englund played Freddy Krueger in the nightmare on Elm Street movies. Needless to say, Patty was freaked out. She didn't believe me at first, but then there was a binder with the hotel info on a table in our room, and Freddy Krueger's face was on it. At night, I joked with her and said that I hope he doesn't come up from the mattress and grab us. She slept with the lights on.

We stayed at an old hotel near the French quarter in New Orleans. Our tour guide told us that we would know when we were on Bourbon Street because there was the smell of urine and throwup. He was right because when we were walking near it, I smelled urine and throwup before Patty did. We ate so many beignets, that it looked like I had a Coke problem. When we visited the Great Salt Lake, the aroma of salt was overwhelming. I couldn't believe that people actually swam in that lake. We took a guided tour of downtown Salt Lake City, and Patty told me that our tour guide looked like Kevin. She took a photo of him and then placed them side-by-side. That was Kevin's doppelgänger.

We took a trip to Nashville because the Foo Fighters had a concert there. Of course, the concert ended up being canceled because someone in the band was sick. Instead, we went and heard a concert at the Grand Old Opry. We also were there when Kenny Rogers got his star on the Walk of Fame in front of the Country Music Hall of Fame. He drove by in a golf cart and Patty said his skin was so tight it looked like Saran Wrap over a tub of fruit salad. OK, she didn't say that, but that's what I was imagining.

We took a cruise from Vancouver to Alaska. When she was six months pregnant with Kevin, we had taken a Cruise to Nowhere. It departed from the port at Penns Landing and then went out into international waters. The cruise only lasted a day and a half. This cruise to Alaska would be seven days. One night Patty and I got dressed up and went to dinner. She had me wear a black suit, white shirt, and black tie. At this time, I had changed from my huge sunglasses to a pair of Blues Brothers sunglasses. I have to say that it looked cool. OK, I have no idea what I looked like. Anyway, after dinner I decided that I wanted to sing karaoke. While sitting in the lounge waiting to sing, some drunk woman walked by and said, "hey, Blues Brothers!". That made me feel real good. Not! When my turn came, Patty walked me up and some asshole yelled out, "Stevie Wonder!". That really pissed me off. Before I sang, I told him that I was not going to sing a Stevie Wonder song. That got a laugh. I killed by the way. I had that crowd in the palm of my hand. Afterwards, Patty and I were in an elevator and a guy got in and said that it would've been funny if I sang a Stevie Wonder song. At this point, I was so pissed off at the rudeness of people. Who the hell were they to say this shit to me? They didn't even know me. Even people that knew me, knew not to say that shit. People are just so goddamn ignorant. I would never say that to anyone.

On our cruise to Hawaii, a young magician came into the audience and was talking about his parents. I had no idea that he was standing right next to us when he said that he was looking for people that reminded him of his parents. Just then, he said, "How about you guys?". At that point, Patty grabbed my arm to help me stand up. Oh dear God. He chose us. I must have stood out like a sore thumb. Anyway, he had us sit at a table on the stage. He proceeded to do this magic trick and when he was done, I said out loud, "Oh my God! I can see". That got a big laugh. Sometimes you just have to make light of the situation

On one trip, we flew into Denver and rented a car. We drove through Nebraska (and yes, a tumbleweed did blow in front of our car) and then into South Dakota to see Mount Rushmore. From there, we drove into Wyoming and then into Yellowstone National Park. We stayed at a large cabin near Old Faithful, and she did not let us down. That was absolutely amazing to hear the force of the water coming up from below. Then we smelled the hot sulfur springs that were coming up from underground. We drove into Idaho on our way into Utah for a few days. We got to listen to an old pipe organ in the Mormon Tabernacle. Patty and I had to be in the car for at least 30 hours and it was so much fun. Just the two of us listening to music and enjoying our beautiful country. I have to admit though that there were times where I was a little uneasy, thinking what if something happened to Patty.

I never thought in a million years that I would visit the state of Oklahoma. However, Bryan went to Fort Sill in Lawton, Oklahoma for his basic training in the Army. Patty and I flew down for his graduation. He told us that he tried-out to sing the national anthem at their ceremony. He did not let us know that he had been chosen, so we were absolutely surprised when he came out and sang the anthem in front of over 200 people. I have to admit that I got a little teary-eyed and choked up hearing him sing. He was so good. It brought back memories of when he was in middle school and high school. Patty and I went to visit the Oklahoma City National Memorial, which is where that crazy man, Timothy McVeigh, blew-up a federal building two years to the day after the Waco Texas compound raid by the FBI.

Walking among the 168 chairs that were in a row in front of the building, was serene and solemn at the same time. Inside the memorial they played a video of the moment when the bomb went off. In the video, you could hear someone talking in a meeting, and all of a sudden hearing this loud explosion. It was massive. Later on we visited Dallas, Texas, and drove the route that JFK and Jacqueline Kennedy drove before he was assassinated by Lee Harvey Oswald. We walked through the memorial on the sixth floor of the school book depository building. We stood on the grassy knoll where Abraham Zapruder took his infamous home movie of the assassination. I had seen that tape hundreds of times over the years, so I knew the view. Patty told me that there were spots on the road where the first, second, and third shots were fired. She also told me how far away the limousine was to the overpass. They were so close from getting away from the shooting. This would be a common theme at every place that we visited. Having the knowledge of seeing the cities on TV and then visiting them. I wish it was under different circumstances, but at least I was there. That sadness that I felt in San Francisco would creep up occasionally, but then as soon as it arrived it would disappear. I never wanted to show my sadness in front of Patty because I did not want to ruin her vacation.

There were mishaps along the way. Like the time that Patty and I were coming out of a restaurant in Redbank, New Jersey, and I tripped on the sidewalk and my cane fell into the street. Instead of seeing if I was OK, Patty walked into the street to grab my cane because she thought that someone would run over it. I was fine by the way. I was getting to be a pro at falling down and not getting hurt. Or the time that Patty made me walk into a telephone pole in New Hope, Pennsylvania. Or the time that Patty was in a rush to get to an elevator before it stopped, and had me punch the brick wall in between the two elevators with my hand. The brick wall won that fight. Or the time that we were in Charleston, South Carolina, and Patty told me to get into a golf court and I banged my head on the roof. Or the time that I fell off into the Grand Canyon. Just kidding.

One of the coolest experiences that I ever had on vacation, was when Patty and I went to Augusta National Golf Course in Augusta, Georgia. For those who are not golfers, this is the mecca for golfers all over the world. It hosts the Masters Tournament every April. The best players in the world come to play this tournament and the winner gets the coveted green jacket, which is put on them by the previous year's winner.

You can't see the golf course from the roads that surround it, so Patty and I stopped at the entrance. There were two older gentlemen at the gate who told us that we were not allowed to stop there. I gave them a bit of an attitude and said that we just wanted to take a picture. They told us that we could park across the street in a parking lot and then come and take a picture in front of the entrance. We did that and as we walked across the street, they noticed that I had my walking cane. We started to talk to them, and then one of the men walked away and then came back to me. He told me that there were video cameras all around and to just act like I am shaking his hand. When I shook his hand, he placed a golf ball in it. How sweet was that? The golf ball was what the professional golfers would use on their practice round. Patty told me that it had green marks on it from the golf course. I thought of my dad and my Uncle Albert. They would play golf every Saturday through their mid-80s. My Uncle Albert was so competitive though. He hated when my dad had a shot in the middle of the fairway, or God forbid, when my dad would beat him. Thank God I was wearing my sunglasses, because I started to tear up.

During a tour of the Alamo in San Antonio, the tour guide gave each of us a headset so that it would be easier to hear him speak while walking among the crowd. As he started to talk, I could not get it out of my head that he sounded like somebody famous. And then it dawned on me that he sounded exactly like Peyton Manning. When the tour was over, I had Patty walk me up to him and tell him who he sounded like. He laughed and said he'd been told that he looks just like Donald Sutherland too.

It seems like each time we walked through an airport and needed to use the handicapped or family bathroom, the door would be locked. We would wait, and then nine times out of ten an airport employee would come out. How disrespectful was that?

We went to a horse farm in Kentucky where they had retired horses, some who had ridden in the Kentucky Derby. Our tour guide drove a golf cart and after stopping at one place to feed a horse, I accidentally got back into her seat. She asked me if I wanted to drive and I said that it would be one hell of a ride if I did.

My big mouth would sometimes get me in trouble because I never knew what people were around me. One time Patty and I were in a train leaving the ballpark in San Francisco, and I spoke out loud about some ignorant people. Patty shushed me and told me that they were sitting right near us. Oops. Another time we were in an elevator with a guy who was staring at me the whole time. Patty told me afterwards what he had done and I told her the next time that happens let me know because I will say to the guy, "What the hell are you looking at?".

We had gotten tickets to the Late Show with Stephen Colbert, so we decided that we would go to New York City early and tour Rockefeller Center. We also went on a tour of Saturday Night Live studios and afterwards the tour guides brought us into a room where we did a mock Tonight Show. I raised my hand to volunteer but they did not choose me. That pissed me off. It got to the end when no one volunteered to be a guest. Patty told them that I could be the guest but then they said that there were lines that I needed to read. She told them that I could just improvise and they relented.

We went to Mackinac Island, which is off the upper peninsula of Michigan, and walked on a path toward the spot where Christopher Reeves and Jane Seymour filmed the movie *Somewhere in Time*. That is Patty's favorite movie and its theme song was what Patty and I danced to at our wedding. We were walking along the path, and Patty screamed out loud and told me that there was a snake on the path. I hate snakes. I almost jumped into her arms.

When we went to the Bahamas, we spent a day at the Atlantis Waterpark. We took a slow ride on the lazy river and then numerous waterslides. This one waterslide was pretty high and Patty decided to go down first. Before she went down, she told the kid that was monitoring all of the swimmers that I was blind and to take good care of me. He must not have heard her because I hit my head on a piece of wood. As I sat there holding my head, he asked me if I was OK. I bit my lip, didn't answer him, and then went down the slide.

The funniest thing that ever happened to us on vacation, happened at Meteor Crater Park in Arizona. There is a large crater in the earth's surface that supposedly was created by a meteor. Patty loves this kind of shit. She told me to sit on a bench while she got close to the crater so she could take a picture. As I am sitting there, I heard someone start to fart. Not just once, but over and over again. This person was farting with each step that they took. I wanted to laugh out loud but I didn't want to embarrass her. For all I knew, it was Patty. For the record, it was not her. When Patty came back, the woman had walked away. I told her what had happened and she did not believe me. We went inside to look at the exhibit, and then Miss Farter walked by us. Patty and I were laughing so hard, but we did not want to laugh out loud. That poor woman. Maybe she had just gotten a colonoscopy. Who knows.

However, hands-down the most embarrassing moment of all our trips, was when we went to the Greenbrier Hotel in West Virginia. This hotel had a replica of the House of Representatives and the Senate chambers where the senators and representatives would have been evacuated if there had been a nuclear attack. Patty and I went for a mineral salt bath. I thought that we would be in the same room together, but boy was I wrong. We went into separate bathrooms and an older gentleman guided me to the locker. Patty had given me a bathing suit to put on, but the older gentleman told me to strip down naked and told me to put on a robe. I felt a little uncomfortable about this but I followed his instructions. He then guided me to a chair outside the room where the mineral salt bath tub was. About 10 minutes later, another older gentleman helped me into the room where the tub was and told me to take off my robe. I felt so awkward. My body at the time look like Montgomery Burns from the Simpsons. Once again I followed his instructions and he helped me into the tub. As if it couldn't get any worse, the older gentleman stayed in the room while I bathed. It was the most uncomfortable I had ever been in my life. When my time was over, and thankfully it couldn't come soon enough, he helped my Montgomery-Burns-looking body out of the tub. The other gentleman then helped me back to my locker where I quickly got dressed. When I got into the hall and saw Patty, I was so pissed off. I told her what had happened and she said why didn't you just wear your bathing suit? I told her that I felt like I did not have a choice. She just shook her head like my dad would always do when I did something or said something stupid. Lesson learned. No more natural salt baths for me. Unless Patty is in the same room.

We went to the top of the Space Needle in Seattle, Washington. What's up with these heights and my wife? We walked on a rotating glass floor with the city of Seattle below us. Thank God I couldn't see because I would probably have had to get a new pair of underwear.

We took a trip to Cleveland, Ohio on our way to Mackinac Island in Michigan. We visited the home where the exterior shots were taken for the classic movie, A Christmas Story. This is the movie where Ralphie wants to get a Red Ryder BB gun but everybody tells him that he will shoot his eye out. I grabbed the BB gun and put it up to my eyes. I always try to find some way to make fun of my vision loss.

It may seem to some that these trips were easy for me. They were not. Anytime you take a trip with a handicap, no matter what it may be, there is always some trepidation. I tried my best to hide that. It's not easy being out in public and being exposed to the world when you have a disability. Even though I could not see, I always felt like I was being watched. My social workers would always tell us that we had to set an example for individuals with vision loss. We didn't want to be that angry person. We wanted to show the world that disabled people can do just as much as anybody else.

Patty and I took a trip to the Bahamas and we got to swim with the dolphins. Well, we put on our wetsuits and stood in water up to our waist while a dolphin swam around us. Even so, it was really cool. It is kind of crazy to let yourself go when you can't see what you are touching. When I could see, my niece worked at this aquarium in Virginia Beach and she allowed us to touch the stingrays. I got a little squeamish about doing that. Now put yourself in my situation where you don't know what you were touching. That happened when Patty and I went to an aquarium in Hawaii and there were stingrays swimming around. She wanted me to touch them and I told her that I didn't want to touch them when I *could* see and I sure as hell am not going to touch them now that I *can't*.

My cousin's wife took my sister, brother, cousins, Patty and I on a memorable trip to Italy. We visited Florence and Rome and it was a trip of a lifetime. I had always wanted to visit Italy. That was on my bucket list.

Even though Patty and I have been all over the United States, I was apprehensive about flying eight hours over the Atlantic Ocean to a foreign country while being blind. Even though I had my family with me, I was concerned about how I would react. On vacation, it was just Patty and I, and I could get pissed off and she would understand or not understand and tell me to knock it off. Would I be able to keep my composure in front of my relatives?

The flight to Italy was long, but I survived. Since my vision was under control and dark, the flight was bearable. Patty watched about three or four movies and I listened to a book and then music. When we arrived in Rome, we climbed on a charter bus on our way to Florence. On the bus ride, my vision started to become completely white--that horrendous whiteness of the headlights of tractor-trailer in my vision. I started to get a headache and then began to get extremely cranky. I started to tell Patty how I was feeling and she told me to keep it down. I was miserable. The thought of being on a bus with my relatives and having to travel four hours to Florence, started to make me panic. I could feel myself starting to tense up and sweat. I fought so hard not to freak out in front of my family. This was the last thing in the world that I wanted to do. It was exactly what I was afraid would happen. I sat in my seat with my head in my hands while everyone on the bus talked and laughed. I felt horrible. Mostly I felt horrible for Patty. She had also wanted to visit Italy and now here we were and I was ruining it.

I did a lot of soul-searching on that four-hour trip. I also did a lot of praying to my mom and dad for strength. There was nothing they could do to make my vision any better, but maybe they could give me some guidance. Slowly but surely I realized that there was nothing I could do about the whiteness. I don't believe that anybody on the bus knew the hell that I was going through except for Patty. I told myself that there were two things I could do. One, I could sit and bitch and be miserable the whole trip and not enjoy myself; or two, suck it up, grin and bear it and enjoy myself with my family. I chose to do the latter. Thank God I did. I'm not saying that was easy to do, but what other choice did I have? Was I going to sit in my hotel room while everybody else was out and about and laughing and having a great time? No way.

So when we ate on the roof of our hotel in Florence and people were talking about the view, I would smile and try to imagine it. When Patty and I walked through the market in Florence, I would just imagine what it looked like. When we drove through Tuscany to a World War II cemetery for American soldiers and Patty told me that it looked just like Arlington National Cemetery, I stood and pictured it in my head.

I did the same when we walked around the Coliseum, the Forum, the Pantheon, Vatican Square, and the Sistine Chapel. I used my ears, with the aid of my hearing aids, to take in all the surrounding sound. I listened to other tourists' reactions to what they were seeing. I listened to Patty describe what the Sistine Chapel ceiling looked like and how beautiful it was.

It was nice to know that all the pressure on this trip was not on Patty's shoulders like previous ones. My family was around to protect us and guide me. I had my cousins and brother to keep watch over me if some unsuspecting pick-pocket artist would try to take advantage of my disability. My sister was my biggest advocate. She protected me like I was a diamond ring. It was nice to know that people had your back. It was a great feeling to know that your family cared so much about your safety. That made the trip so much easier. They took me under their wings and guided me.

The hardest part about being on vacation is going to the bathroom. Not necessarily me not being able to urinate, but finding my way around a bathroom in either a strange hotel room or out in public in a strange city. Sometimes we would be in two or three different hotel rooms during a vacation and when I got up in the middle of the night to go to the bathroom, it could get confusing. Sometimes I thought I was still at home or other times I thought I was in a previous hotel room. One hotel room had a step going down into the bathroom. I almost killed myself.

Going to bathroom in public can also be entertaining. Patty and I went to see a show at the Kimmel Center in Center City Philadelphia. At intermission, we went into the lobby and Patty walked me toward the men's room. I had my walking cane with me and my sunglasses on. As I started to walk into the men's room, a man came from behind me and grabbed my arm to help me. He asked me if I needed to go to the stall or the urinal and I told him I needed to go to the urinal. Now, there is an unwritten rule in men's rooms that men do not talk or look at each other while they are urinating next to one another. This guy must have not read the memo because he started to talk to me while standing next to me at the urinals. He asked me if that was my wife or girlfriend outside. He asked me if I lost my vision during the war. I answered no. At this point, I was done and I turned around to leave the urinal and he asked me if I needed my hands washed. I quickly answered no, and got the hell out of the bathroom.

Another time I needed to go to the men's room at an airport in New Orleans. Patty opened the door and told me where the urinals were and I followed her instructions. When I was done, an airport employee helped me to the sink to wash and dry my hands. He then led me out of the men's room. I thanked him and shook his hand. He responded by telling me that he was 75 years old. I thought that was kind of an odd answer.

Another time in an airport bathroom, another airport employee helped me but he did not speak any English. That was comical. As I came into the men's room, he said something and I just shook my head yes. I kind of thought that he had asked me if I needed a urinal. When I got done, he again said something and I shook my head yes because I thought that he asked me if I needed to wash my hands. Then when I was done washing my hands, he said something and I shook my head yes because I knew that he wanted me to dry my hands. How about that? A blind man communicating with another man in a different language.

After a while, I didn't care if I went into a ladies room or not. It was also easier for Patty to not have to open up a men's room door and tell me where the urinals were. We went to Churchhill Downs and Patty took me into the ladies room with her. We are standing in the ladies room waiting for a woman to come out of a handicap stall, and another woman walks into the ladies' room. She then looks at Patty and me, then goes back out of the ladies' room and looks at the name on the door. I guess she was confused and had to make sure that she was going into the correct bathroom. Patty and I were on a cruise to Hawaii and rather than going into the men's room, she took me into the ladies' room. After we were both done, Patty took me to the sink to wash my hands. At that point, a woman came and said to Patty, "you do know that this is a ladies' room?". No shit, Sherlock. Of course Patty knew that this. She wasn't the blind one, I was. One time Patty led me into a men's room and I thought that I was standing at the urinal. I unzipped my zipper and almost started to urinate, when I realized that this was not the urinal but the sink. How funny would that have been if someone had walked in at that point and saw me urinating in the sink. I could just blame it on my being blind.

So Johnny, you and I have been everywhere. I could not have wished for a better traveling companion. Can you imagine how difficult it would be if you had to take a blind person to Center City Philadelphia for an eye visit? Now times that by 10 and imagine how difficult it must have been for Patty to travel with a blind person all over the country and then to Europe. As difficult as it was for me to travel, I really don't believe that I could have done what Patty did. I don't think that I would have the strength and confidence in myself to accomplish all that she had with me. Is it harder to travel blind or is it harder to travel with a blind person? I don't really know the answer. I know how it is from my perspective but I have no idea what it's like for Patty. Ask yourself, could you do that? Would you be able to handle someone who is completely reliant on you? Could you handle driving from Denver, Colorado, through Nebraska, up to South Dakota, through Yellowstone National Park, down to Utah, back to Wyoming, and finally back to Denver with a blind person in the passenger seat not being able to guide you? Not many people could do that. Then again, not many people are tough as nails like Patty. I would not want to have any other person in this world be my travel buddy.

Just because I lost my vision, didn't mean that Patty and I could not travel anymore. At least that's what she told me.

Chapter 20 - Jelly Donut

Like I had said before, being the youngest of six children was like being an only child. My Mom was in a bowling league on Tuesdays and I would go with her and stay in a room with the other children, eating a jelly donut while she bowled. I loved them so much back then, but today I can't stand them. When my son and my daughter-in-law told us in 2018 that they were expecting in August 2019, Patty and I were over the moon thrilled with excitement.

For their gender reveal, they were going to get donuts that were either filled with blue cream or pink cream. That was an issue for me since I would not be able to see the color and therefore not be able to know the sex of the child. Their solution to this problem was for my donut to be a jelly donut for a girl and a cream-filled donut if it were a boy. Simple enough solution, right? My son and daughter-in-law had their families over to their house for the gender reveal. It was very exciting. I was sitting on a couch with my sister to my left and Patty to my right. I was given my donut and I could tell that it was heavy so I thought in my head that it was going to be a boy. On the count of three, everyone bit into their donuts. The problem was when I bit into my donut I just got dough. Then I took another bite and could not decide if it was jelly or cream. Now I'm going to keep you in suspense on the gender of their child.

Among all the issues that I was trying to come to terms with about losing my vision, one of the most important ones was not being able to see my grandchildren. I know how much my Mom and Dad loved their grandchildren. They loved when their grandchildren came over to their house to hunt for Easter eggs, and how much they loved taking care of them when Patty and I went on vacation. How would my grandchildren react to their PopPop being blind? Would I be able to watch them without people being concerned for their safety? Would they be embarrassed of me in front of their friends? I wouldn't be able to do with them, the same cool things that my Dad did with us--like having us sit on his lap while he drove his tractor across our backyard or while he drove a go-cart up and down our neighborhood street. I had always dreamed about throwing a ball around with my grandsons or watching my granddaughter play soccer. Sadly though, this would more than likely not be the case. How was I going to cope with this loss?

As with everything in my life, this issue came up numerous times in my low-vision groups. The women at the Center put my mind at ease and told me that it did not matter that I could not see because my grandchildren would love me unconditionally. They should know because they had grandchildren of their own. Like I had said before, one of the women in my low-vision and adjustment-to-blindness group took care of her grandchildren when they were babies. This helped me out a little bit, but I was still upset at the possibility that I would not be able to do the same things with my grandchildren as my Mom and Dad had done with theirs.

I was 13 years old when my sister gave birth to her first child. I was hoping that she was going to have a boy, but when I found out that she had a girl, I was so mad at her. I distinctly recall sitting in her hospital room and not making eye contact with her because I was pissed-off that she did not have a boy. That feeling of anger lasted until I held my new niece. She was so cute and beautiful. One year later, I would be pushing her around Ocean City, New Jersey in her stroller. Up and down all the sidewalks and making wheelies with the stroller to make her laugh. When I brought Patty over for the first time to meet the whole family, my niece was six. She was so protective and jealous, that she sat right next to Patty and gave her dirty looks during the whole meal. She still does that today. Just kidding.

My sister then had another little girl, but this time I was not so pissed-off. She was just as cute and beautiful, although her personality is much different than my first niece. One time I took her to the local store to get her a toy and I played a song by Bryan Adams called "Diana". I was singing this song and telling her that this song was about her. I thought that she would laugh, but the opposite happened. She started crying and then telling me to turn off the song. Oh shit. Then I brought her into the store and told her that she could get any toys that she wanted. That was a big mistake. She pointed to an ape and told me that she wanted that. I looked at the price and then told her are you sure you want to get this one? How about another one? Well, she screamed and then I relented and got that one for her. Nice uncle that I am.

When my cousin was around 2- 1/2 years old, he pointed-up to my armpits and told me that I had a mustache growing. My other cousin, a girl, once sat on my lap when she was around the same age and asked what this bump was. Oddly enough, that would be what Patty said to me on our first date. Just kidding. When my other sister was pregnant, she told me that I was going to be the godfather. I was so honored and could not wait to meet my godchild. She was so cute as well but, she was a kleptomaniac. My Mom had this toy bin at her house and my godchild would always steal something and bring it home. I was so proud of her. Little Oliver Twist--actually, the artful dodger.

I was always so fond of my nieces and my little cousins. They were so cool to hang around with. Now how would my grandchildren react to me around the same age? I didn't know, but I knew that I would love the hell out of them regardless.

So getting back to the jelly donut...after my second bite, I didn't know if it was jelly or cream. Then my sister leaned into me and asked me if I knew what it was and I told her to wait a second. Then I realized that it was a jelly donut and I was going to be a grandfather to a little beautiful girl. Everybody was so happy. Which kind of makes me wonder if they would have reacted any differently if it were a boy. Would somebody say, oh shit, it's a boy? No.

On the night of August 22, 2019, I held my beautiful Rowan Jane Savini in my arms for the first time. My family told me that they had never seen me so happy before. They were right. I was so excited to be holding such a precious little baby. A gift from God. She grabbed onto my index finger and it melted my heart. All my apprehension that I had about being a grandfather and not being able to see my granddaughter, disappeared. I could hold my granddaughter. I could smell my granddaughter. I could hear my granddaughter. It didn't get any better than that.

They always say that you become much more mellow as a grandfather than you are as a father. They are right. As a father, each time my child cried, it got me uptight. When Rowan cried, I thought it was the cutest sound in the world. I would protect her with every fiber in my body just like I protected my own kids. She was in my heart forever.

When my son and daughter-in-law brought Rowan to our house for the first time, I picked her up and walked her all over the home, into each room and whispered very quietly in her ear. When she got a little rambunctious, I would sing softly in her ear. Just like I always did with my own kids. She has the cutest cheeks. They are so large and I would lean my cheeks up against her cheeks. We literally danced cheek to cheek. When she cried, PopPop would come to the rescue.

As Rowan got older, she started to crawl and I would get down with her and put my hand on her back to make sure that she would not bump in to anything. Basically, I was doing the same thing that any parent or grandparent would do with their grandchild, but rather than watching them with their eyes, I was watching them with my hands. Honestly, I probably was more protective of her since I could not see. Most grandparents or parents nowadays would occasionally look at their phone or the TV when their child is crawling around, but with me I didn't have any phone or TV to look at so my top priority was making sure that Rowan was safe by placing my hand on her. I have a phone case on my belt and Rowan is so smart because she knows that's where my phone is. She loves to hear music and she will come over to me, climb up on my lap and put my hand in my phone clip and pull my phone out. I will put music on for her and then she grabs my phone and crawls or walks away. This is really good for me to know where she is at all times. If the music is fading away, then I know that she is either walking or crawling in the hallway to her room.

The cutest moments so far were when she walked in the hallway to her room and sat down next to the door that was closed. I crawled after her because she had my phone in her hand and I knew where she was located. As I got next to her, I sat down and started to tickle her. She laughed and then slowly stood up from a seated position and proceeded to fart. I thought that was the funniest thing ever. I started laughing out loud, and then she started to laugh out loud. How immature am I? Laughing at my granddaughter farting.

When my kids were young, I would read them Sesame Street books and make believe that I was talking like Elmo, Grover, Big Bird, and so on and so on. With Rowan though, this was going to be an issue because I could not see. So I would pick up a book and start making up stories about her and then turn the pages. Sometimes you have to improvise when you are blind. I know right now at the age of two, that Rowan has no idea that I cannot see her or does not understand what a blind person is, but when she gets older I will sit her down and tell her what it is like. Just like my great niece asked me when she was three years old; "why can't you see?". I know the day will come that I will have to tell Rowan. Hopefully, by the time that she gets old enough to understand, they will have come up with a cure for blindness. I do know this though, she will be empathetic and compassionate for those with disabilities. That is something that I will instill in her. Accept everyone for who they are. I might not be able to hold her hand and guide her down to the water on the beach, but that does not mean that I can't hold onto her hand and she can guide me down to the beach and go into the ocean. The roles will have to be reversed for now.

When Kevin FaceTimes us, I can't see Rowan's reaction to me, so I have to ask Patty if she is smiling. As of right now, she only speaks a few words so I cannot communicate to her over the phone. I accept what I am given by her as a blessing. It makes me feel good to know that she recognizes her PopPop. To be honest though, it really does suck that I can't do the same things that my brother and sisters can do with their grandchildren. Hopefully they don't take this for granted , because it all can change in a flash. I wish that I could drive my grandchildren to the playground, just the two of us, and push back-and-forth on a swing, then afterwards take them to get some ice cream and sit down at a park bench and just act goofy with them. My father would fake like he was going to pour soda onto Emily, and one time he finally did. Emily was so shocked and my Dad just laughed out loud. Now if I try to do that with my grandchildren, I probably would throw the soda on to Patty and that would not be a good idea. Although my grandchildren would be laughing, I would have to pay big-time for pouring soda on Patty.

I have my Dad's wedding ring. When Kevin got engaged I asked him if he wanted his PopPop's wedding ring and he said that he did. The problem was that my Dad had massive fingers, but Kevin's not so much. So we brought the ring to the jeweler and had it sized-down to fit Kevin's finger. I asked the jeweler if there was any way that he could keep a piece of the ring so I could put it on a necklace around my neck. So now that's what I have on my neck. On the back of the gold, I have my Dad's initials, I wear it on my necklace next to an Italian horn and Jerusalem cross medallion that my Mom brought back from her trip to Israel. Whenever I hold Rowan, she knows that I have those three items on my necklace and she takes the chain out from under my shirt and plays with them. Whenever she does that, I think of the piece of my Dad's wedding ring and how she is touching a piece of my father. That makes me feel really good and occasionally puts tears in my eyes.

When Kevin was in Boy Scouts, his troop took a trip to the Franklin Institute in Philadelphia. I went with him and stayed the night. There was a machine that you could look into and it showed you what you would look like when you got older. I did it and damn did I look bad. Now that I can't see, I still have the memory of how I looked on that day. So when I get out of the shower and I brush my hair, I realize that I don't have as much hair as I used to have, I think back to how I looked in that machine. When I feel my face starting to droop a little bit, I think back to how I looked in that machine. However, I do not know what Rowan looks like. Patty and the kids have told me that she looks like Kevin when he was younger. That helps me out a lot. When I try to think about Patty, I think of how she looked the first time I saw her in Montreal. I think back to a picture that I took of her on her 21st birthday in the kitchen of the old Cape Cod home with my Mom and Dad next to her. I think about our engagement picture. I think about how she looked walking down the aisle on our wedding day. I think about the photos that we took on our honeymoon in Niagara Falls, where we are on the cover of a magazine and the caption says "world's cutest couple". I think of the photo that we took of our family golf outing, where we are standing side-by-side with our golf clubs crossed over one another. By the way, she won the "worst Savini golfer" on that day. I think of how she looked when she was pregnant with Kevin. I think about how she looked when she held Emily for the first time. I think about how we all looked standing on the beach in Virginia. I think about how we all looked in the photo in Colorado with the lake behind us and the Rocky Mountains in the background. When you lose your vision, all you have to hold onto are the memories. I know that Patty and the kids have aged, just like I did in that machine at the Franklin Institute. They are still the same people but look slightly different.

Rowan will age just like my kids have done. There will be many times in her life that she will fall down, and I will be there to tell her to get back up again. Life can be unfair at times, but that does not mean that you let life take hold of you and keep you down. It didn't with me and it won't with my grandchildren. I am lucky.

Early in 2021, we gathered at my son's house in New Jersey for another gender-reveal party. Was it going to be a boy or a girl? Did it really matter? Of course I would love to have a grandson to carry on the Savini name. At this point though, I am lucky to be a grandparent. So I sat in my chair at the kitchen table and awaited the countdown. I then bit into the donut and this time instead of it being jelly it was custard. I thought it was a boy but then I was told that it was a girl. I didn't care. I was so happy. Even though I don't care for jelly donuts, the jelly donut that I ate on Rowan's gender-reveal party, was the best jelly donut I ever had. I will be so excited to hold baby Marnie just like I was to hold baby Rowan. The same protective measures that I have in place for Rowan, I'll use for Marnie. I will always have a hand on her back when she is crawling or walking. I will have both hands on her when she is sitting on my lap. I will know where she is at all times because my music will be playing on my phone in her little hands. I may not know what she looks like, but I do know that she will be my granddaughter and no one can take that away from me. Early on the morning of July 10, 2021, Patty got a phone call from Kevin telling her that Ashley was having contractions. Just as on the morning of September 28, 2012, when Patty received a phone call from my sister telling us that my father was passing, this was a phone call at the same time but under different circumstances. Whereas with my father we were saying goodbye to him, we were now saying hello to Marnie.

In 2012, Patty and I quickly got dressed and drove the hour and a half to my father's nursing home. On that day, my vision was so white and I sat in the backseat with a blanket over my head. In 2021, I sat in the front seat with Patty and my vision was just as white as it was back in 2012. Sitting next to my father's bed as he passed away, I had tears in my eyes. Standing next to my daughter-in-law's bed and holding Marnie in my hands for the first time, I also had tears in my eyes. She was as light as a feather.. 7 pounds and 1 ounce. I told Patty that it was like holding a bag of cotton balls. My sunglasses were off and I was looking at her but all I could see was whiteness. A tear started to form in my right eye and I wiped it away with my thumb and then dried it on her blanket. They were tears of joy and of course sadness.

Patty was holding Marnie and she sat down on the couch and had Rowan in her other arm. She introduced Rowan to Marnie and Rowan kissed Marnie. Brought me back for the first time when we brought Bryan home from the hospital and Emily held him. I told Kevin that Bryan had gotten him a gift and Kevin was so confused. He was almost 4 years old but he was too smart to be fooled that an infant actually got him a gift. What had happened almost 28 years to the day of Bryan coming home, was playing in my mind while Rowan was saying hello to her little sister for the first time. I put my sunglasses on so that no one would know that I was tearing up. Maybe they saw me, maybe they didn't.

There is a picture of my Dad holding my second niece in the backyard of the old Cape Cod. He is of course wearing his white, V-neck T-shirt with the sleeves cut off. He is pointing at the camera and looking at my niece. It is one of the cutest pictures ever taken. Of course when my Dad was a young father, he scared the crap out of all of us. When he became a grandfather, just like my grandfather and all grandfathers, he had mellowed out. Whenever his granddaughters or grandsons started to cry, they would run to their PopPop for a hug. The weekend when Marnie was born, Rowan would run to her PopPop whenever she was crying or being scolded. It's crazy how life imitates itself. I was the one who disciplined our children when I was a father and now here I am all mellowed out as a PopPop just like my Dad. I really miss him.

Kevin carries with him at all times a white handkerchief that was my father's, and rosaries that were my mother's. The night before they brought Marnie home, they were having a tough time with her and the hospital nurses were not very nice to them. Kevin is not a very religious person, but on this night he took out the rosaries and handkerchief and asked my Mom for help. It must've worked because in the morning a much nicer nurse came in and helped them out. Thanks, Mom. I miss you too.

Chapter 21 - This Isn't the Bathroom

When I was around 14 years old, I would turn off the sound during a Philadelphia Eagles football game and act like I was the announcer. Of course, during the mid- to late-70s, the Eagles were absolutely horrendous. I distinctly remember the Eagles playing the Los Angeles Rams on Monday Night Football and the fans were carrying around a huge dog bone with *Beagles* written on it. That game, the Eagles lost 42–3. I used to listen to the Philadelphia Flyers on my radio in my bedroom in the mid-1970s. This is when they were really good and won consecutive Stanley Cups. One of the announcers, Gene Hart, was announcing a Philadelphia Flyers hockey game against the Montréal Canadiens. The Flyers were playing absolutely awful and Gene Hart was getting pissed-off. He actually said that the Flyers were playing shitty. Another Philadelphia Flyers announcer Don Earle, actually said the forbidden word on a broadcast. One of the Philadelphia Flyers hit the goal post and Earle said the following: "Flyers just hit the fucking post." He never announced another Philadelphia Flyers game.

In the basement of the old Cape Cod, I remember watching the Philadelphia 76ers during the championship season in 1982–83. I would sit down on that black and white checkered couch and dribble a basketball back-and-forth between my legs while watching a game. That was a season for the ages. They were awesome. Every game they would end up beating their opponent by at least 15 points. I had a notebook next to me and I would keep stats for all the players. For instance, tracking each player's points, assists, and rebounds. When the 76ers finally won the championship that same season over the Los Angeles Lakers, I cried. I was almost 20 years old and had been following the 76ers since I was 13.

The Philadelphia Phillies always frustrated me. From 1976 to 1978, they would lose in the playoffs in the most unbelievable ways. During a playoff loss in 1978, I kicked a hole in my wicker hamper. What preceded that burst of anger is when Garry Maddox dropped a line drive to centerfield and Ron Cey, nicknamed "the penguin" because he ran like a penguin, danced happily down the third-base line to score the winning run. In 1980, the Phillies had a magical year and won the World Series. My brother-in-law took me to game six when the Phillies beat the Kansas City Royals at old Veterans Stadium. Afterwards, while sitting in traffic on Pattison Avenue in my brother-in-law's Datsun B210, the fans were rocking the car back-and-forth.

Why am I telling you all about the Philadelphia sports teams? Well, I was, and still am, a Philadelphia sports fanatic. The problem though is when I lost my vision, watching the games was just not the same anymore. In the old days, no matter what the sport, the announcers would tell you everything that was going on during the game…the score, how much time was left, the inning, and what quarter or period. However in the present, that just is not the case. It got to be so frustrating, that I just would listen to the games on the radio because they described more of the action. Listening to a game on TV, no matter the sport, it always seems like they are having a conversation with each other and not telling you what is going on. Sometimes, while I am watching a basketball game for instance, I will have to grab my phone and ask what the score is. That's how bad it gets. Try doing this sometime. Turn on a sporting event and then close your eyes and tell me if you know what the hell is going on. I sure can't and most people who are legally blind, or completely blind, can't figure out what is going on either. I sometimes get so annoyed and yell at the TV. If I ever came across one of these announcers in person, I would tell them that I really don't give a shit what your favorite movie is or what the hell you ate for dinner last night, just tell me what the hell is going on in a game. I don't know when this whole "not talking about what is going on in the game" first started. Maybe it started before I lost my vision and I just never noticed, but I really doubt it. What I used to once love watching, has now turned into somewhat of a nightmare for me. It has taken away the joy of watching a basketball game or football game or whatever sport.

Going to a sporting event is another issue. I used to take Kevin to the Philadelphia Flyers for one game a year when he was around 10 years old. There is a really cool picture of us in our Flyers jerseys. It was taken in the kitchen of the Langhorne house. We would drive down early and get hoagies from Wawa and then sit in the car and eat them before going into the Wells Fargo Center for the game. There is another picture of Kevin and me when he was around four years old at a Philadelphia Phillies game at Veterans Stadium. We are six rows behind home plate and it was another really cool picture. I had both of those pictures on the wall at my desk. Years later, Kevin took me, Patty and Ashley to a minor-league baseball game near his house. At this point, I was blind and it was definitely a unique situation. He had to tell me what was going on. He had to tell me when it was a ball or a strike. Whenever the ball was hit and it came back near us, it scared the shit out of me. Before when I could see and there was a foul ball headed my way, I would prepare myself to grab it. I really miss those days. It's the little things that you miss the most when you can't see. So going to a sporting event is not something that I will ever enjoy as much as when I could see the action. Yes my kids could tell me what is going on, but it's just not the same. When I go to a concert, at least I can hear the band and I don't need Patty to tell me what song they are playing.

Watching a TV show sometimes can be a nightmare because I don't know what is going on. I have to ask Patty and she hesitates because she is watching the show and can't tell me what is going on and listen to the show at the same time. Early in 2016, digital cable switched over to audio description. They were supposed to do it for all TV shows, but that was not the case. This becomes an issue whenever Patty and I want to watch a movie. If the movie does not have audio description, then we just don't watch it. I figured out a workaround for this problem. I will read the book before we watch the movie so I know what is going on. We did this with the Godfather so Patty did not have to give me any play-by-play.

Going to the movies at a movie theater sometimes can be a problem as well. Within the past five years or so, movie theaters have given a headset to people with vision impairment. This is similar to watching a TV show at home with the audio description on. With the headset, the audio description of the movie is being played. It actually describes the beginning of the movie when they are showing what movie company released the movie. It tells you everything that is going on. It gets a little uncomfortable when I am watching a sex scene at home with audio description with Patty and the kids. It tells you everything and I mean everything.

During every one of my talks in front of grade-school children, the same question gets asked over and over again. Can you read braille? The answer to that is no. I cannot read braille because there really is no reason for me to learn how to read braille. We are extremely fortunate to have amazing technology for blind people. You can talk to your phone and your phone will answer your command. It could tell you to text someone or call someone. It will tell you what the weather is for a specific day. You can look up how tall or how old a famous person is. Basically it can tell you anything you want to know. This also applies to my iPad. This is my life source. Without it I would be completely lost and bored. My iPad plays my music and it is where I can listen to Sirius XM radio, go on Facebook, listen to podcasts and so on, and so on, and so on. I can also listen to books.

When I started to slowly lose my vision, I had a sense of where everything was in my home so I never really got hurt. This all changed when I completely lost my vision. I had to learn to adjust. I started to count the number of steps from my bedroom door to the top of our stairs. Then I counted the number of steps down to the first floor to our foyer. This continued from the foyer into the family room. I would use my palms, back of my hands, forearms, elbows, feet, hips, or ass to guide me around the house. By doing this, it prevented me from banging into walls and allowed me to know what direction I was going. However, this did not prevent me from having accidents in my own home. Going to the bathroom sounds like a very simple thing to do. However, I can't remember the amount of times that I bang my head on the bathroom counter while taking off my shorts or pants. I once hit my head on the kitchen counter so hard, that I cut my forehead. I would like to say that I saw stars, but I didn't. It just changed a different color in my vision. Almost like a strike of lightning across a black sky. I hit that counter so hard in the kitchen that it knocked me onto my back. If I ever get murdered, and I sure hope I never do, it will be so easy for the coroner to know who I am by the amount of bruises and bumps I have on my shins. At least 100 times I have walked into a coffee table, end table, bed frame, toilet, car or any other inanimate object. It seems like every time I bump into a table and knock something down, the first question out of Patty's mouth is; what did you knock down? I always get a kick out of that question because how would I know what the hell I knocked down.

One time, Patty, the kids and I came home from one of my siblings' homes and they all went upstairs. I had to go to the bathroom, so I grabbed the door to the bathroom and opened it up… at least I thought it was the bathroom. I reached into what I thought was the bathroom, and I started to slide down backwards on our basement's wooden steps. To this day, I don't know how I didn't kill myself. When I put my hand out, I grabbed onto the wooden railing and for some reason it turned my body backwards and I slid down standing up. I slid all the way down to the bottom step. Patty and the kids heard the loud banging all the way upstairs and ran down as fast as they could. Patty was screaming are you OK, are you OK? After sliding all the way down the stairs backwards. I slowly walked up the stairs as if nothing had happened, but my heart was beating 1000 beats a second. Patty and the kids asked me how I could have opened up the basement door not knowing that it wasn't the bathroom. I had no answer for that. This is something that I did thousands of times when I could see, and when I couldn't. For reasons unknown to me, this particular day I opened up the basement door instead. I was one lucky soul on that particular night.

Losing my vision didn't mean that I lost my sense of humor. Every night when I went to bed, I would open up Emily's door and act like I was going into the bathroom. She always got a kick out of this. Then she would scream, Dad! And then I would act like I thought I was in the bathroom instead of her room. I obviously cannot stand and pee like I used to. If I did, more urine would get on the wall than in the toilet. So I have to pull the toilet seat down and sit on it. For some unknown reason though, my sister put the toilet seat up when I was at her house one time. I felt like telling her, seriously? Do you really think a blind man stands up to pee? I don't think so. At least I didn't pee in her sink. Or did I? She will never know.

We had a hard cover on our in-ground pool. Supposedly, this hard cover could hold an elephant on top of it and it would not collapse. One winter, there was about 10 inches of snow on top of the cover. I took our ten pound maltipoo dog out on his leash in the backyard. Even though our back yard had a PVC fence surrounding it, Patty was nervous that the dog would crawl under the fence. I took our little guy out to go to the bathroom and ended up on the pool cover. I don't know how this happened. Luckily I had my phone with me and I nonchalantly called Emily. When she answered, I said calmly, I am on the pool cover. No less than three seconds later, Emily came flying out of our three-season room and put out her hand to guide me off of the pool cover.

The incident with the pool didn't stop during the winter. I had my incidents with the pool during the summer as well. Our pool was a rectangular shape and it had steps in the shallow end. One summer evening, the kids were out and Patty and I were getting ready to go into the pool. We had rafts on our deck and we were bringing them towards the pool. Normally when I would go to the pool, I would walk until I hit the couches and then I would know where I was located on the pool deck. Sometimes I would slowly walk to the pool on the grass and then work my way up to the steps into the pool. Once again, for some unknown reason, I didn't walk to the pool like I normally did. I had let my guard down and I guess I got a little too cocky. The next thing I knew, my foot did not touch concrete but it touched air and then it fell into the pool. My left foot got caught underneath itself and scraped the concrete and coping around the pool edge. It bent my leg back and when I fell into the water I did a half somersault onto my back. I thought I had broken my left leg. That's how much pain I was in. I was screaming and Patty had no idea what had happened. All she knew was that when she was on the deck I was walking towards the pool and then all of a sudden I was in it. I slowly made my way to the steps and felt the railing and climbed out. Fortunately I was not seriously injured. All I had was a nasty scrape on my knee and foot. Another time I was doing yardwork around the pool. I had put in a walkway from our deck to the pool and then a walkway parallel to the pool to where the filter was. In between the steppingstones I put down white rocks. This didn't prevent weeds from growing in between them though. Weeds can grow anywhere. This particular evening, I grabbed a lid from one of our trash cans and used it to put the weeds in. I went into the house to get a drink of water and when I came out I grabbed the lid that was next to the deck and started to walk the pathway to the pool. I knew how many stones I had to walk before I got to the concrete lip that's around the pool area. I guess I got a little too cocky again and bolted out of the three-season room, grabbed the lid and started to walk quickly to the pool area to continue my weeding. Next thing I knew I was in the pool. Dumb ass! Not only was I in the pool, but the trash can lid and all the weeds that I had picked up were in the pool with me. This time I was fully clothed. Once again I found my way to the railing in the shallow end of the pole and slowly walked out. My body was dripping as I walked into the house. Patty and Emily were in my in-law's addition with the door open. I probably looked like the creature from the Black Lagoon. I stood there and yelled Patty's name. When she came out and saw me, she asked me what happened? Seriously? You really need to ask a man who is completely soaked in water what happened when we have a pool in the backyard and I did that stupid shit before?

The physical ailments will heal but they will leave scars. The scars you can see. The scars that you can't see are the ones that are caused emotionally. What I mean by that is, when you get hurt because someone that you were close to, or thought you were close to, does not reach out to see how you are doing.. this causes the most pain for anyone who is going through a tough time no matter what the case may be. When you have friends, you think your friends will be there forever. Friends come and go though. Sometimes it's because you change jobs or you change where you live. Sometimes you are friends with the parents of your children's friends because you see them at sporting events or they're on the same teams. I had a close friend where I worked and when I got fired, she never reached out. That really hurt me a lot. I know that when I am friends with you, I am friends to the end. Not like blood brothers bullshit or anything like that, but I never try to do anything that would hurt you. I followed the golden rule, do unto others as you would have done to you. It's funny that that was preached to us when we were growing up in the Catholic Church, but then when you meet people of the same religious belief as yours, they don't follow through with what they were taught. You always hear people say to you when you were sick or going through a tough time, let me know if there's anything I can do. I know that I said that before I lost my vision. It's such a bullshit statement, isn't it? Let me know if there's anything I can do for you? Like someone who is going through a hard time is going to call someone up and say to them, "hey, remember when you said to call you if there's anything that you could do for me? Well, I'm calling you now. Mow my lawn". What you should say to someone who is disabled or going through a hard time is the following: I will call you next week to see how you are doing or I will text you next week to see how you are doing. You better follow through with it too. People will hold you to that and if you don't call, they will never rely on you again.

When I was working, I would walk to the other side of the building and sit in these lounge chairs overlooking the parking lot. At that point, I had a flip phone. I would take out my phone and text my sisters, brother and nieces to see how they were doing. It didn't take that long to do it either. Yes I was busy, but I took 10 minutes out of my day and out of my lunchtime to reach out to see how they were doing. Now none of them was going through anything serious mind you. Do I expect them to text me every day to see how I am doing? Of course not. They all have busy lives. Would it be nice if I received a text once a week? Of course. Everyone would love to hear from someone once a week to see how you are doing. It lets that person know that you were thinking of them. I still try to do that to this day.

What I am going through is nothing compared to those who are going through cancer or have survived cancer or those whose loved ones have not survived cancer. I know a loved one who has survived cancer and one who has not. I have seen a loved one beat cancer into remission and then have it come back again 10 years later. I have seen a loved one lose their hair and their energy. It is a horrible sight and I wish that on no one. Not even my worst enemy. Unfortunately, a loved one was not fortunate enough to survive cancer. Anyone that goes through cancer, in my opinion, is a strong person. Just because you lose your battle, does not mean that you didn't fight real hard to survive. That's why when someone is going through a horrible illness or a rough time, I never say to them: "let me know if there's anything I can do". I hate that and I hated that when I was going through my depression. Don't say anything, just do it. What happens when someone says that they will call you and they don't, destroys a person inside. Believe me, it's happened to me on numerous occasions and still does today. I just lost my vision. Imagine what it is like for someone who is going through cancer. This type of shit has happened to me with family members and I will just leave it at that and move on.

The second time that I met Kevin's wife, I had on a pair of khaki shorts and a T-shirt. Kevin went up to his room to get something and it was just me and Ashley in the family room. I figured I would take this opportunity to get to know her better. We talked for about five or ten minutes and then Kevin came down and then they both left. As I got up from the couch, I realized that my zipper was down the whole time. Oops! Dumb ass. The second time I met Bryan's girlfriend, was on the day that he was moving out of his apartment. I was wearing a sweatshirt and blue jeans. I sat down on the couch and she walked over and we both started talking. When it was time for us to leave, I stood up and realized that my zipper was down. What the fuck is up with me and my zipper being down all the time? Actually, if my memory is correct, my zipper was down the first time I met Patty. Just kidding but maybe that is good luck.

Once when my daughter was sitting on the couch with her fiancé, I was lying on the floor and I put my hand out and started to rub what I thought was her foot. The problem was that it wasn't her foot. I was rubbing the foot for a while before my daughter's fiancé said, "that's my foot". How embarrassed was I? It didn't stop there though. Patty, Bryan, Emily, Evan and I, went to see Hootie and the Blowfish at Hershey Stadium. Bryan was off to my right and Emily was next to Bryan, then Evan was next to Emily. During one of the songs, I put my arm out to my right and started to rub what I thought was Emily's arm. I even made a comment that her arm was smooth. Problem was that it wasn't Emily's arm, it was Evan's. Thank God that I only have three children because if I had four, and my fourth child brought home her or his significant other, I probably would be brought up on harassment charges.

One time I was standing next to Patty in line and I put my hand out and thought that I was touching her back. I wasn't touching her back but I was touching her front. And when I mean her front, I literally was feeling her up. Patty didn't believe me when I said I thought it was her back but I really thought it was. Thank God she didn't slap me across the face. Thank God it was Patty and not some unknown stranger. Another time we were at Kevin's in-law's house and we were getting ready to say goodbye. I stood up and walked over to shake Kevin's hand and while shaking his hand I said to him, goodbye asshole. Problem was that I was not shaking Kevin's hand but I was shaking his brother-in-law's hand. Thank God Kevin's father-in-law did not hear me say that or he probably would've punched me in the face. Everyone laughed and got a kick out of it. I never laughed so hard in my life.

All of my life I was always expecting things to be handed to me. I thought that I would be a really good sports announcer but I never put the preparation, dedication or motivation into it to succeed. In fact I never really even tried. I thought that I would be really good on the radio and I tried it out for a year and a half or so, and then quit. I never wanted to put in the time or energy to succeed. Basically what I'm saying is I was always lazy. Also, you could say that I was afraid of failure. I thought I was weak and that feeling of weakness probably reverts to when I worked at that private country club and I fucked up so many times I can't even remember. That probably gave me low self-esteem but I probably already had that to begin with. I never attempted to overcome that feeling. This feeling of failure followed me into the workplace as I got older. I never wanted to take risks and I never put enough faith in myself. It prevented me from advancing within the company.

However, when I got to the point where I lost my vision, I could have thrown in the towel and said this is it. I'm never going to come out of this depression and I'm going to sit on the couch for the rest of my life. Those thoughts of low self-esteem crept into my mind over and over again…while I was sitting on the couch alone or when I was lying in bed wide awake not being able to get back to sleep. During the mini panic attacks that I had or the bouts of anxiety that led me to thoughts of suicide, I could've thrown in the towel. The loneliness that I felt sitting in the dark in my bathroom on the cold tile floor crying my eyes out because I was so scared of what the future held for me. The many times that Patty drove me to Wills Eye Hospital for an emergency visit, or up to Boston for the depressing news that I received. The many many many many times that I considered putting a hole through a wall because I was so frustrated and angry at the world. The dozens of lyrics that I wrote depicting how angry, frustrated, resentful and sad I was with the loved ones around me. Losing my mother, father, uncle, my job and my vision within a one- year span could've knocked me on my ass forever. It all comes down to the one quality that I thought I never had growing up or as an adult. That is strength.

The strength that my mother told me that I had during our visit to the medium in New Jersey. She knew what I didn't know at that time, that I was tough. I resisted her plea because I thought she was lying. I thought she was just trying to say something to make me feel good about myself at one of the loneliest points and darkest moments of my life. However, over the course of the last nine years, I realized that I had a strength deep inside of me and in the lower reaches of my soul that I never knew existed. I've been knocked down so many times in my life by my vision loss, and each time I got back-up only to be knocked back down again. This cycle continued over and over for the past 20 years. I am not naïve to think that the rest of my life will be full of highs without any lows. That is not the case. There is an old saying that says you have to look on the bright side of everything that comes into your life. Well, here goes the bright moments of losing your vision. I was given the gift of being able to talk to young children about what it is like to show empathy and compassion. I was able to show them what it is like to lose your vision and then keep on going. I was able to show them that just because you have some adversity in your life, doesn't mean you give up. I learned to appreciate Patty for the wonderful woman that she has always been. I have learned not to be so damn tough on my kids and to appreciate what great children I have. Most importantly though, I had to lose my vision in order to see more clearly.

Epilogue

I am sitting in Patty's grandfather's chair in the third bedroom of our
townhouse. We call this room the music room because this is where I
practice playing guitar. My guitar is off to my right on its stand. It is
a Yamaha acoustic guitar that was given to me by my guitar teacher before
he left to play lead guitar in a band on a cruise ship. Unfortunately, this
occurred in March 2020 and then the pandemic arrived and shut everything
down. I started to take lessons in March 2019 and came in with an old
beat-up acoustic guitar. I am left-handed so I needed to have the strings
restrung in order for me to play. I play every now and then. I know the
basic chords, but that's as far as it goes. I once thought that I was really
good, and recorded myself on my phone. When I played it back, I was
absolutely horrified by how bad I was.

In front of me is an exercise bike that my company gave me for my 20th
anniversary. I ride it every now and then, but I should ride more than I do.
It overlooks the window onto the townhouse across the street. Patty once
bought a tandem bike, thinking that we could ride this bike around the
neighborhood. It sat in its box for two years until Patty gave it to Kevin for
an auction at his high school. I eighty-sixed the idea of having us put that
bike together and driving it around our neighborhood. I could just envision
us crashing into a stop sign. I thought that it would be cool if we got a
surrey like they have on the boardwalk, with Patty in the front peddling
and me in the back listening to music. Kind of like our version of driving
Miss Daisy, but it would be called driving Mr. Dennis.

On August 31, 2020, Patty and I left our Langhorne home for the final time. We had bought a townhouse in York, Pennsylvania on Valentine's Day of 2020. With the kids out of the house, it got to be too much for us to maintain our house and the pool. She decided that she wanted to retire and I reluctantly agreed. We both thought that the Langhorne home would be our forever home, just as I'm sure my Mom and Dad thought that the old Cape Cod in Newtown Square would be their forever home. I walked around the house before we left that morning, going into each room and trying to remember a good memory that happened. I did the same thing the last time I walked through that old Cape Cod home in Newtown Square. It's funny how life comes full circle. Now I was turning another chapter in my life book. I knew my way around that Langhorne house like the back of my hand once I lost my vision…knowing the number of steps to each room and when to turn to go into a hall. It was going to take time to learn the layout of our new townhouse.

Life is about how to adapt and adjust to the curveballs that it throws our way. This was going to be no different than learning how to live without vision. I was saying goodbye to the friends that I had made at the Adjustment to Blindness Center. These were my peers and also my heroes. I had learned so much from them. Ironically, the first month Patty and I were in our new home, we ordered a pizza and pulled in front of the pizza place. A man started to walk towards our car and Patty told me to roll down the passenger door window. The man came up and asked if we were his Uber. Patty said that we were not and he kindly thanked us and walked back to the front of the pizza place. Patty then told me that the man was blind. She went in to get our pizza and when she came back into the car she asked if we should see if he wanted a ride home. I told her that that would be the right thing to do. She got out of the car and asked him if he needed a ride home and he said yes. He got in the backseat of our car and our little 10 pound multipoo was so excited to see him that he sat on his lap. We got into a conversation and he told us that he worked at the pizza place and that he had been blind since he was 15 years old. He lost his site in a boating accident on the Schuylkill River. He was now 47 years old and was living with his brother and sister-in-law in York. We started to talk about the Philadelphia Eagles, and then he asked if Patty and I were married. Patty said yes and then told him that I was also blind. He did not believe her until I had him feel my cane. How crazy is that? We met somebody who was totally blind and who needed a ride home. Patty and I then started to think how wrong it was that he was sitting there for 45 minutes and nobody in the pizza place drove him home. How courageous this man was to wait outside for an Uber driver. Think how scary it must have been for him waiting there all alone. Could he have trusted that Uber driver to not rob him? Could he have trusted us not to take advantage of him? He was such a kind man and I felt so horrible for him. He had lost his vision when he was a teenager and I lost my vision when I was 47 years old. He had such a great attitude though. Courageous man. God bless him.

Sitting on Patty's grandfather's chair in the music room, I dictated into my iPad my thoughts that I had kept inside for over 20 years. These were thoughts that I never imagined that I would remember because I thought I had forgotten. Bringing back the painful memories of losing my vision and hitting rock-bottom is not an easy thing for me to talk about. Especially talking about my Mom, Dad, and sister, was tough as well. Going back in time and navigating what had happened to me in such a short span, was a little uneasy. I never realized how much I lost in just one short year. The loss of my mother, my father, my job, and then finally my vision. I think that would be tough for anybody to endure. This is nothing in comparison to what other people have had to go through in their lives. I still am able to walk which allows me to travel with Patty. I have my hearing which allows me to go to concerts and enjoy the music. If you ask a person who is blind if they would rather be blind or deaf, their answer would be blind. If you ask a person who is deaf, if they would rather be blind or deaf, they would tell you deaf.

As painful as writing this book was for me, it was also therapeutic. It made me realize how far I had come and how strong I really am. It made me realize how many lives I had touched. You never know who's watching you. I could not have completed this book without the help of my wife Patty and my Aunt Marianna. The thoughts and everything that is written in this book is my own account in my own words. After dictating a chapter in the Notes Application of my iPad, I would give it to Patty to have her correct any misspellings or miss-pronunciation that Siri had misunderstood. After Patty would make the corrections, she would forward the chapter to my aunt for grammar and punctuation corrections. My aunt is the self-proclaimed grammar queen. After receiving the corrections from my aunt, Patty would put the corrected chapter into a word document on my iPad. This process continued all throughout the book. I started dictating this book in the beginning of March 2021 and completed it in the middle of August. Most of the time before I started a chapter, I knew what I was going to talk about. Other times, it was almost as if someone went inside my body and started to speak for me.

What is in store for me for the rest of my life? I now have two beautiful granddaughters to love, and hopefully in the future many more grandchildren. I look forward to walking Emily down the aisle in August

2022. Hopefully I don't knock anybody over. Patty and I are going back to Italy and will travel to Indiana, Missouri, and Illinois this coming fall. After my last doctor's appointment, I was told there is a possibility--as slim as it may be--that in the near future I may be able to get some sort of vision back. When patients are born deaf, doctors can insert a cochlear implant to bypass that part of the ear so that they are able to hear. Since my optic nerve is so damaged, there really is nothing they can do to bring back my vision. My eye doctor told me that there is a procedure that can bypass your optic nerve and implant a retinal chip into the back of your eye. This will allow people to get some of their vision back. The reason why I said a slim possibility, is because I have had so much damage to other parts of my eye, besides my optic nerve. My retina has a lot of scarring on it and with the advanced glaucoma that I have, pressure in my eye will always be an issue. If I never see for the rest of my life, I can accept that. Like I had said before, other people have gone through worse and are still going through worse.

I hope that I explained what it is like to lose your vision and then to live as a blind person. I try to reveal every part of me in this book-- the good, the bad, and the ugly. Adding humor to a very serious subject, is how I live my life. Reading this book, I hope it gave you a new perspective on anyone with a disability. I will end this book explaining a song that I wrote in the midst of one of the darkest times of my life. The song is written about a man who loses his wife/girlfriend, whether it be to a breakup or death. I tried to write lyrics that were both non-fiction and fiction. The song is exactly that. It's talking about a fictional subject but in reality it's about me losing my vision. Thank you once again and God bless.

Blind

By: Dennis Savini

[Verse 1]

When flowers are planted

I never see them grow

When the rain stops falling

I don't see the rainbow

When the leaves change colors

I'll never really know

I'll never see the light

I live in the shadows

[Chorus]

The day that you left me

Is the day I went blind

Without you in my life

There's nothing I can find

Should have seen the signs

Read between the lines

Without you in my life

I might as well be blind

[Verse 2]

I don't see the robin

When it's making its nest

I don't see the sunrise

And I don't see it set
I don't see the stars shine
Their beauty I forget
My heart won't let me see
It's filled with much regret

[Chorus]
The day that you left me
Is the day I went blind
Without you in my life
There's nothing I can find
Should have seen the signs
Read between the lines
Without you in my life
I might as well be blind

[Bridge]
You don't know what you love
Until it's lost
Your love I took for granted
And now I pay the cost

[Chorus]
The day that you left me
Is the day I went blind
Without you in my life

There's nothing I can find
Should have seen the signs
Read between the lines
Without you in my life
I might as well be blind

Made in the USA
Middletown, DE
12 November 2021